SimQuick

PROCESS SIMULATION IN EXCEL

SIMQUICK

PROCESS SIMULATION IN EXCEL

David Hartvigsen

Mendoza College of Business Administration
University of Notre Dame

Prentice
Hall

Upper Saddle River, New Jersey 07458

To Nancy

Executive editor: Tom R. Tucker
Assistant editor: Jennifer Surich
Production editor: Christy Mahon
Manufacturer: Victor Graphics, Inc.

Prentice
Hall

ISBN 0-13-065148-6

10 9 8 7 6 5 4 3 2 1

Table of Contents

Preface

Motivation

Process simulation is one of the conceptually simplest and most often applied techniques in Operations Management and Management Science, yet it has not been widely taught to business students. A key reason for this is that performing process simulation requires the use of software, and the software that is available tends to be complex and expensive. Even the more graphics-based packages, although often beautifully designed, frequently have an enormous number of features that place an unnecessary burden on students (and instructors) in classes that are not devoted to simulation.

SimQuick is a computer package for process simulation that is easy to learn (most of its features can be learned in under an hour of class time or independent reading) and inexpensive. It is aimed primarily at business students (and managers) who want to understand process simulation and be able to quickly analyze and improve real-world processes. SimQuick is flexible in its modeling capability; that is, it is not a "hardwired" set of examples; it requires true modeling. In addition, SimQuick runs in the widely-known Microsoft Excel spreadsheet environment (it is an ordinary Excel 97 file with some hidden macros). Hence, users of Excel will already be familiar with much of the interface, and the results are already in the spreadsheet, ready for analysis.

This booklet accompanies SimQuick. It presents the basics of process simulation by having the reader construct, run, and analyze simulations of realistic processes using SimQuick. Chapter 1 contains a brief introduction to process simulation and the concepts underlying SimQuick. The next four chapters contain a variety of examples of process simulation. These examples are organized as follows: waiting lines (Chapter 2), inventory and supply chains (Chapter 3), manufacturing (Chapter 4), and project management (Chapter 5). Each example is followed by an exercise. All the examples and exercises have been designed with business students (and managers) in mind.

In addition to presenting the basics of process simulation, this booklet introduces a number of *key concepts* from the analysis of processes: service level, cycle (or waiting) time, throughput, bottleneck, batch size, setup, priority rule, and so on. The booklet also introduces some *key trade-offs* from the analysis of processes: number of servers vs. service level, inventory level vs. service level, working time variability vs. throughput, batch size vs. service level, and so on. These notions are presented through computer models that the reader constructs and experiments with using SimQuick.

How to use the booklet

The booklet is self-contained; that is, all technical terms involving processes or operations are defined. (The reader is assumed to have a rudimentary understanding of how to use Excel on the level of knowing how to save files and how to enter information into cells.) The chapters are organized around typical topics in Operations Management and Management Science courses so that this booklet can easily be used in these types of courses.

The reader should first read Chapter 1 (which contains a conceptual explanation of process simulation and SimQuick) and Section 1 of Chapter 2 (which contains a step-by-step explanation of how to use SimQuick by completely working through a simple example). The remaining sections in Chapter 2, as well as the sections within Chapters 4 and 5, can be read in any order. However, the sections within Chapter 3 build on one another and should therefore be read in sequence.

The bulk of Chapters 2 through 5 consists of examples of processes that can be modeled using SimQuick. When needed, an example discusses how to build the SimQuick model. Each example is followed by an exercise.

The booklet contains three appendices. Appendix 1 contains tips on how to enhance SimQuick by using some of the features built into Excel. These tips are tied to examples in the booklet. Appendix 2 describes how to use an advanced feature of SimQuick called Custom Schedules. Appendix 3 contains a succinct description of all the features of SimQuick and can be used for reference. Hence, the features of SimQuick are presented in two ways: through examples and in a reference manual.

Solutions to exercises: Instructors are provided with complete solutions (in Excel) to every exercise. These solutions may be distributed to the students at the instructor's discretion.

Web site: Refer to **www.prenhall.com/hartvigsen** for additional information on SimQuick, this booklet, technical support, and process simulation in general.

I have used SimQuick in the classroom with Executive MBAs, full-time MBAs, and undergraduate business students. After a one-hour introduction in class (basically, reviewing Section 1 of Chapter 2), the students are able to solve a variety of modeling problems with little help. This introduction also serves as a launching pad for term projects, whereby students identify and analyze real-world processes of their choice.

Acknowledgments

The design of SimQuick was inspired by the breakthrough simulation product XCELL, so I want to begin by acknowledging its authors: Richard Conway, William L. Maxwell, John O. McClain, and Steven L. Worona. Next, I want to thank my editor Tom Tucker at Prentice Hall. He has been indispensable in helping me to define this project and bring it to fruition. I also want to thank the following reviewers for their careful reading and excellent suggestions: Sue Abdinnour-Helm, Arundhati Kumar, Larry Meile, Kelly B. Nichols, Jeffrey L. Rummel, and Billy M. Thornton. I only wish there was more time so I could implement more of their ideas (perhaps for the 2nd edition!). I want to thank my colleague Lee Krajewski for a number of discussions of pedagogy in general, and process simulation in particular. I want to thank Kristin Ann Steffeck for her copy editing. Finally, I want to thank my many students (Executive MBAs, full-time MBAs, and undergraduate business students) of the past two years who have served as guinea pigs and made many helpful suggestions during the development of this software and booklet.

Chapter 1: Introduction

Learning objectives:

- To understand the idea of process simulation
- To understand the general structure of SimQuick models
- To understand the role of uncertainty in process simulation
- To get SimQuick running on your computer

Overview

This chapter contains a brief definition of process simulation, an overview of how SimQuick works, and instructions for how to run SimQuick on a computer. Most of the details of how to use SimQuick are covered in Chapter 2, Section 1.

Section 1: What is process simulation?

Process simulation is a widely used technique for improving the efficiency of processes. Following are some examples of processes and some related efficiency problems that can be addressed with process simulation (and SimQuick):

Examples of processes:

- People moving through a bank or post office
- Telephone calls moving through a call center
- Parts moving along an assembly line or through a batch process or a job shop
- Inventory moving through a retail store or warehouse
- Products moving by trucks, trains, or ships through a supply chain
- A software development project

Examples of efficiency problems:

- How many tellers are needed to keep waiting times at a bank reasonably short?
- What effect will a new answering system have on how long customers wait at a call center?
- What effect will a new just-in-time (JIT) inventory system have on the number of units produced per day on an assembly line?
- What is the best batch size to use in a factory?
- What is the best delivery policy for goods at a warehouse?
- How much inventory should be kept on the shelves in a grocery store?
- How many machines should each worker operate in a manufacturing cell?
- How should inventory be distributed along a supply chain?
- What is the expected duration of a software development project?

With process simulation, you begin by building a computer model of a real-world process. Your initial goal is to have the computer model behave similar to the real process, except much more quickly. You then try out various ideas for efficiency improvements on the computer model and use the best ideas on the real process. Thus, a lot of time and money can be saved.

Simulation is particularly useful when there is uncertainty in a process (e.g., the arrival times of customers, the demand for a product, the supply of parts, the time it takes to perform the work, the quality of the work). With uncertainty, it is often difficult to predict the effects of making changes to a process, especially if there are two or more sources of uncertainty that interact.

Section 2: What does SimQuick do?

SimQuick allows you to perform process simulation within the Excel spreadsheet environment. There are three basic steps involved in using SimQuick:

1.   Conceptually build a model of the process using the building blocks of SimQuick (introduced below).

2.   Enter this conceptual model into SimQuick (this is done by filling in tables in a special Excel spreadsheet).

3.   Test process improvement ideas on this computer model.

The building blocks in SimQuick are *objects, elements*, and *statistical distributions. Objects* typically represent things that move in a process: people, parts in a factory, paper work, phone calls, e-mail messages, and so on. *Elements* typically represent things that are stationary in a process. There are five types of elements:

Entrances: This is where objects enter a process. Entrances can represent a loading dock at a warehouse, a door at a store, and so on. You must specify when objects arrive at an Entrance and in what numbers (using a statistical distribution or an explicit "custom" schedule).

Buffers: This is where objects can be stored. Buffers can represent a location in a warehouse or factory where inventory can be stored, a place where people can stand in line at a post office, a memory location in a computer for e-mail messages, and so on. You must specify how many objects a Buffer can hold.

Work Stations: This is where work is performed on objects. Work Stations can represent machines in a factory, cashiers in a store, operators at a call center, computers in a network, and so on. You must specify how long a Work Station works on an object (using a statistical distribution).

Decision Points: This is where an object goes in one of two directions. Decision Points can represent the outcome of a quality control station, different routings in the processing of a mortgage application, and so on. You must specify a rule for deciding in which direction an object goes (using a statistical distribution).

Exits: This is where objects leave a process. Exits can represent a loading dock at a warehouse, a customer buying a product at a store, and so on. You must specify when objects depart from an Exit and in what numbers (using a statistical distribution or an explicit "custom" schedule).

The third building block, *statistical distributions,* is discussed in the next section.

A SimQuick model describes how the objects move between the elements. You have a great deal of freedom in constructing models using the building blocks of SimQuick; hence, you can model a variety of real processes. However, because the number of building blocks is small and they are simple, some complex real-world processes will be difficult to model in SimQuick. For such situations, a more powerful simulation package may be needed.

When a SimQuick simulation begins, a "simulation clock" starts in the computer and runs for the designated duration of the simulation. While this clock is running, a series of *events* sequentially takes place. There are three types of events in SimQuick: the arrival of objects at an Entrance, the departure of objects from an Exit, and the finish of work on an object at a Work Station. Whenever an event occurs, SimQuick moves objects from element to element as much as possible. SimQuick keeps track of various statistics during the simulation (e.g., the mean inventory at each Buffer) so you can analyze what happened when the simulation is over.

Section 3: How does SimQuick incorporate uncertainty?

As in a real process, the timing of events in SimQuick can be uncertain or random. Here is an example: Suppose you are entering a model into SimQuick that contains a Work Station. You must specify how much time this Work Station works on an object. What do you do if this time varies in a random fashion at the real work station? A typical approach is to observe the real work station and record a list of real working times. Here are three common possibilities and the ways in which SimQuick models them.

Case 1: The list of real working times has a "bell-shaped" histogram:

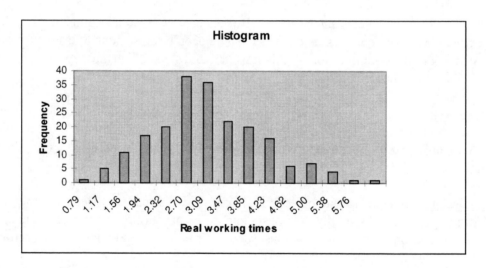

Then, a list of numbers taken randomly from a normal distribution, with the same mean and standard deviation as your list, is likely to have a similar-looking histogram. So, for example, if your list of numbers has a mean of 3 minutes and a standard deviation of 1 minute, then you would enter Nor(3,1) into SimQuick. Thus, you are instructing SimQuick to randomly pick each working time for this Work Station from the normal distribution with mean of 3 and standard deviation of 1.

Case 2: The list of real working times has a histogram that is "skewed to the right" as follows:

4

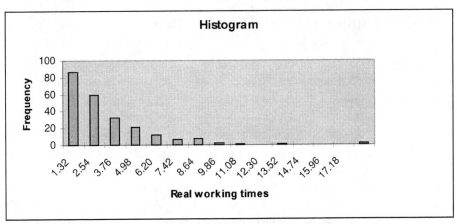

Then, a list of numbers taken randomly from an exponential distribution, with the same mean as your list, is likely to have a similar-looking histogram. So, for example, if your list of numbers has a mean of 3 minutes, then you would enter Exp(3) into SimQuick. Thus, you are instructing SimQuick to randomly pick each working time for this Work Station from the exponential distribution with mean of 3.

Case 3: The list of real working times has a histogram whose bar heights are all roughly the same:

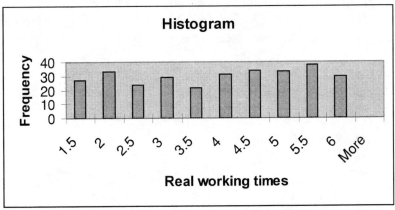

Then, a list of numbers taken randomly from a uniform distribution, with the same minimum and maximum values as your list, is likely to have a similar-looking histogram. So, for example, if your list of numbers has minimum and maximum values of 1 and 6, then you would enter Uni(1,6) into SimQuick. Thus, you are instructing SimQuick to randomly pick each working time for this Work Station from the uniform distribution with minimum and maximum values of 1 and 6, respectively.

The details of how to use the "Nor," "Exp," and "Uni" functions are provided in Chapters 2 through 5 and Appendix 3. To input other distributions (or fixed schedules), see Appendix 2.

Section 4: System requirements and "installation"

System requirements: To run SimQuick, you must be able to run Microsoft Excel on your computer (Excel can run from your hard drive or from a network). In particular, you need to have Excel 97 or later on either a PC or a Macintosh.

"Installing" and running SimQuick: The disk accompanying this booklet contains a file called "Simquick.xls." It is a standard Excel spreadsheet file (with some special worksheets and hidden macros). To use SimQuick, simply launch the application Excel and, within Excel, open your copy of Simquick.xls (see note below). You are now ready to go!

It is probably most convenient to put a copy of Simquick.xls on your computer or network space and to open this copy when you want to use SimQuick.

Note: When opening Simquick.xls, you may see a window with the message: "The workbook you are opening contains macros..." If this occurs, just click the "Enable macros" button.

Mac users: You may have to allocate more memory to Excel. If this is necessary, you will be informed when you run SimQuick.

Saving a SimQuick model: After opening Simquick.xls, you may save your work at any time just as you do with any Excel spreadsheet: Simply click on "Save As" under the "File" menu, rename Simquick.xls., and specify a location on your computer or network space.

If a problem arises with your copy of Simquick.xls (e.g., the formatting gets changed or a worksheet gets deleted), just replace it with a fresh copy from the disk that accompanies this booklet.

Chapter 2: Waiting Lines

Learning objectives:

- To understand the basics of using SimQuick
- To model, simulate, and analyze a variety of waiting line processes
- To understand the following performance measures: service level, mean cycle (or waiting) time, and mean inventory (or number of customers in line)
- To analyze the trade-off between number of servers and service level
- To understand the SimQuick elements: Entrances, Work Stations, Buffers, and Decision Points
- To understand the advanced SimQuick features: resources and priorities

Overview

In this chapter, we consider waiting line processes (also called queueing systems). In a typical process of this type, customers arrive at a service in a random fashion. They may be arriving at a bank (as in our first example), a fast-food restaurant, a car wash, or even via the phone at a 1-800 customer support center. After arriving, the customers typically get in a line, wait awhile, and then are served in some way. They may then leave the process or get in another line to be served again later. Management is typically interested in determining the right number of servers or adjusting the time to serve customers so they don't have to wait too long and so the fraction of customers able to enter the process is sufficiently high. Hence, the key performance measures of *mean cycle* (or *waiting*) *time* and *service level* are introduced in this chapter.

The first section of this chapter discusses a simple waiting line process: a bank. This section is a "must read" because it contains a thorough description of how to use SimQuick and most of its features. In particular, this section shows how to model a process with SimQuick elements, how to enter a model into SimQuick, how to run a number of simulations, and how to analyze the results. The SimQuick elements called Entrances, Buffers, Work Stations, and Decision Points are introduced. The second section contains a number of examples that illustrate the variety of waiting line processes and associated issues that can be modeled with SimQuick. Examples involve a grocery store, a fast-food restaurant, a call center, and a department of motor vehicles.

The third section of this chapter introduces two advanced features of SimQuick: *resources* and *priorities*. With these features, more complex waiting line processes can be modeled. This section contains examples of two fast-food restaurant processes.

Section 1: Solving a problem with SimQuick

Example 1: A bank

Consider the following process within a small bank: customers enter the bank, get into a single line, are served by a teller, and finally leave the bank. Currently, this bank has only one teller working at a time. Management is concerned that the wait in line seems to be too long during the peak hours from 11 A.M. to 1 P.M. Therefore, they are considering two process improvement ideas: adding a second teller during the peak hours or adding a new ATM machine inside the bank.

Modeling the process (with a process flow map)

We first construct a *process flow map* of the bank using the elements of SimQuick (see below). This is a conceptual step, so it can be done anywhere you prefer (e.g., on a piece of paper or on a computer). (The map below was made using some simple drawing tools within Excel; see Appendix 1 for details.) The flow map for the bank contains four elements, which are represented by boxes. For each element, the top line indicates the element type and the bottom line is a name (we follow this convention throughout the booklet). In this case, objects represent people and the arrows on the map indicate how the objects move between the elements. Note that the final element is a Buffer called Served Customers. An object entering this Buffer corresponds to a customer leaving the bank. The Buffer gives us an easy way to count our simulated served customers. You might have expected to see an Exit here, but with an Exit, objects leave the model according to a specified schedule instead of when they are ready to leave. (For example, an Exit can be used to model finished goods leaving a factory on trucks that depart periodically according to a schedule; Exits are introduced in Chapter 3.)

Process Flow Map for Bank

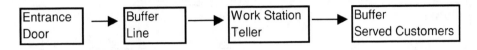

Entering the model into SimQuick

We're now ready to start entering our model into SimQuick.

Launch the application Excel on your computer and, within Excel, open your copy of the Simquick.xls file. This file is on the disk accompanying this booklet; you can copy it or save it to your computer or network space (see Chapter 1, Section 4, for details). You should see the following screen, which is called the Control Panel:

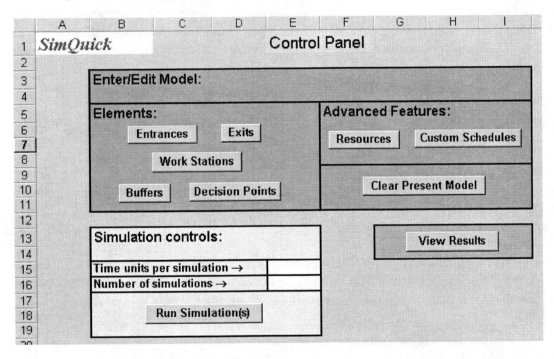

You can save your work at any time. To do so, click on "File" in the menu and then "Save As." Enter a new name (usually something to remind you of the process you are modeling) and designate a location on your computer or network space.

Observe that there are a number of buttons on the Control Panel. In particular, there is one button for each type of element. We will be clicking on these buttons to enter information for each element in our model. This can be done in any order, but let's do it in the same order that the objects move. So click on the "Entrances" button. You should see the following screen:

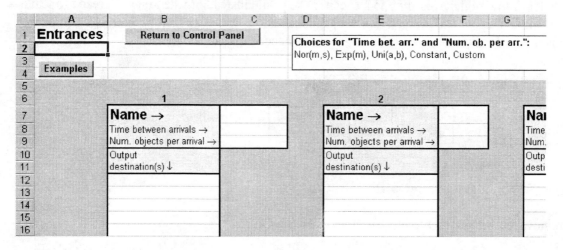

For each Entrance in your model, you must fill in one table (working from left to right). So let's fill in table #1. To begin, type Door into the "Name" cell.

In the next cell down, we specify when objects arrive at this Entrance. Traditionally, this is done by specifying the amount of time between arrivals. To do this, suppose we have spent some time observing the door of our bank and have compiled a list of actual times between customer arrivals. We discover that this list of numbers has a mean of 2 minutes and a histogram with the same shape as an exponential distribution. (Thus, customers tend to arrive at the bank every 2 minutes.) The interarrival times of customers can then be approximated by numbers, generated randomly, from an exponential distribution with a mean of 2. Thus, we enter Exp(2) in this cell. (In general, interarrival times of people at services can often be closely approximated by the exponential distribution.)

In the next cell down, we specify how many objects arrive at a time. In this case, let's assume people usually arrive at the bank one at a time; thus, we enter a 1 here. (If there was uncertainty about the number of objects entering, we could enter one of our three distributions; in this case, SimQuick would round to give integers.)

Next, we specify where objects go after this Entrance. From the process flow map, we see that objects go next to the Buffer whose name is Line, so under "Output destination(s)" enter Line (these rows should be filled in from the top down). The table should now look as follows:

1	
Name →	Door
Time between arrivals →	Exp(2)
Num. objects per arrival →	1
Output destination(s) ↓	
Line	

Now click on "Return to Control Panel," followed by "Buffers." You should see the following screen:

	A	B	C	D	E
1	**Buffers**	**Return to Control Panel**			
2					
3	Examples				
4					
5					
6		1			2
7		**Name** →			**Name**
8		Capacity →			Capacity
9		Initial # objects →			Initial # ob
10		Output	Output		Output
11		destination(s) ↓	group size ↓		destinatio
12					
13					
14					
15					
16					

In table #1, enter the name Line. In the next cell down, we must specify the maximum number of objects that can fit into this Buffer at one time. This is a small bank, so let's say we can estimate this size as 10. So enter 10. The next cell down asks for the initial number of objects in this Buffer. This is an estimate of the number of people in the line at 11 A.M. Let's say that over a number of days we observed a mean number of five people in line at 11 A.M. So enter 5. Now we have to specify where objects go next. In this case, they go to the teller, so enter Teller here. You are also asked to specify the "Output group size." Because people leave the line one at a time, enter a 1 here. If people were leaving the line two at a time, then you would enter a 2 here (this feature is useful when, for example, you are putting objects into batches in a factory). The table should look as follows:

1	
Name →	Line
Capacity →	10
Initial # objects →	5
Output destination(s) ↓	Output group size ↓
Teller	1

If, at some time during the simulation, an object arrives at the Entrance and the Buffer is full (i.e., it contains 10 objects), then the object does not enter the process. Furthermore, it does not enter the process later in the simulation; hence, it effectively goes away. For our bank example, this represents a customer who arrives at the bank but immediately leaves because the line is too long (this is sometimes referred to as *balking*).

Now, click on the "Return to Control Panel" button followed by the "Work Stations" button. You should see the following screen:

	A	B	C	D	E	F	G	H
1	**Work Stations**		Return to Control Panel					
2					Choices for "Working time":			
3					Nor(m,s), Exp(m), Uni(a,b), Constant			
4	Examples							
5								
6			1					2
7			**Name** →				**Name** →	
8			Working time →				Working time	
9		Output	# of output	Resource	Resource		Output	# of output
10		destination(s) ↓	objects ↓	name(s) ↓	# units needed ↓		destination(s) ↓	objects ↓
11								
12								
13								
14								
15								
16								
17								

In the first table, enter the name Teller. Next, we describe the "Working time" of this teller. Let's assume we have observed tellers in action for several days and discovered that their service time per customer can be approximated by numbers, generated randomly, from a normal distribution with a mean of 2.2 minutes and a standard deviation of .5 minutes. So enter Nor(2.2,.5) for the "Working time."

For "Output destination(s)," enter Served Customers. For "# of output objects," enter 1 because people leave the teller one at a time. (If, for example, this Work Station represented a machine that split objects into identical pieces, then we would enter a bigger integer.) The final two columns are not relevant for this model, so you can leave them blank. The table should look as follows:

	1		
	Name →	Teller	
	Working time →	Nor(2.2,.5)	
Output destination(s) ↓	# of output objects ↓	Resource name(s) ↓	Resource # units needed ↓
Served Customers	1		

Now click on the "Return to Control Panel" button followed by the "Buffers" button. In table #2, enter the name Served Customers. For the "Capacity," just enter a big number that is sure to exceed the number of customers served from 11 A.M. to 1 P.M. For this example, 100 will do the job, but SimQuick allows the capacity to be as large as 10,000. Enter 0 as the "Initial # objects." These objects have no output destination, so the Buffer tables should look as follows:

1			2	
Name →	Line		**Name** →	Served Customers
Capacity →	10		Capacity →	100
Initial # objects →	5		Initial # objects →	0
Output destination(s) ↓	Output group size ↓		Output destination(s) ↓	Output group size ↓
Teller	1			

Click on "Return to Control Panel."

The Control Panel contains the last two cells to be filled in. "Time units per simulation" asks us for the duration of each simulation. Because each simulation is two hours and the time units we have been using for the Entrance and Work Station already refer to minutes, enter 120 here.

Note: In general, a time unit in SimQuick can represent any real time interval: 1 second, 3.5 seconds, 1 minute, 1 hour, 2.5 days, and so on. However, time units must be used consistently throughout a SimQuick model (in all statistical distributions and in "Time units per simulation").

"Number of simulations" asks us for the number of times we want to simulate the 2-hour period. Because each simulation is based on randomly generated numbers, each simulation can yield different results. Hence, you typically want to do more than one simulation and to analyze the results by using means (and possibly some other statistics). For now (to simplify the display in this text), let's do only five simulations; so enter 5. This part of the Control Panel should look as follows:

Simulation controls:	
Time units per simulation →	120
Number of simulations →	5
Run Simulation(s)	

General principle: As the amount of uncertainty in a model increases (i.e., the number of statistical distributions used and the amount of their variability), the number of simulations should increase.

We are now ready to go, so click on the "Run Simulation(s)" button. It will probably take a few seconds (this depends on the speed of your computer). It will take longer as you increase the number of elements (maximum of 20 of each type), the time units per simulation (maximum value 100,000), and the number of simulations (maximum value 100). Some messages will appear (in

13

the lower right portion of the Control Panel), telling you what SimQuick is doing. SimQuick will "beep" when the simulations are successfully completed.

If SimQuick seems to be taking too long, you may hit the Esc key at any time to abort. If SimQuick is running after 30 seconds, then a window will open asking you how you want to proceed.

If you made some typing mistakes, then SimQuick will indicate where the problem is with an error message. You should correct the problem and then hit "Run Simulation(s)" again. A common mistake is entering an "Output destination" for an element that is not exactly the same as the "Name" of the element where you want the outputs to go. (Watch for extra spaces at the end, and make sure uppercase and lowercase match.)

Interpreting SimQuick results

When the simulations are complete, click on the "View Results" button. You should see a table similar to the following, although the exact numbers will probably be different because SimQuick generated random numbers during the simulations.

Simulation Results								
Element types	Element Names	Statistics	Overall means	Simulation number(s)				
				1	2	3	4	5
Entrance(s)	Door	Objects entering process	57.00	61	54	59	56	55
		Objects unable to enter	7.40	13	7	10	1	6
		Service level	0.89	0.82	0.89	0.86	0.98	0.90
Work Station(s)	Teller	Final status		Working	Working	Working	Working	Working
		Final finished inventory	0.00	0	0	0	0	0
		Mean finished inventory	0.00	0.00	0.00	0.00	0.00	0.00
		Mean cycle time (fin. inv.)	0.00	0.00	0.00	0.00	0.00	0.00
		Work cycles started	55.20	57	54	54	55	56
		Fraction time working	0.99	1.00	1.00	0.96	1.00	1.00
		Fraction time blocked	0.00	0.00	0.00	0.00	0.00	0.00
Buffer(s)	Line	Objects leaving	55.20	57	54	54	55	56
		Final inventory	6.80	9	5	10	6	4
		Minimum inventory	1.40	1	2	0	2	2
		Maximum inventory	10.00	10	10	10	10	10
		Mean inventory	6.77	7.98	6.62	6.36	5.65	7.24
		Mean cycle time	14.70	16.80	14.72	14.12	12.32	15.52
	Served Customers	Objects leaving	0.00	0	0	0	0	0
		Final inventory	54.20	56	53	53	54	55
		Minimum inventory	0.00	0	0	0	0	0
		Maximum inventory	54.20	56	53	53	54	55
		Mean inventory	26.74	28.34	26.16	26.28	26.10	26.83
		Mean cycle time		Infinite	Infinite	Infinite	Infinite	Infinite

Although, for the most part, the meaning of these results may be obvious, it's worth discussing them in detail one time. In addition to summarizing the behavior of the model over time, the results also allow you to track down every object that was present during each simulation.

The first two columns contain the element types and names in the SimQuick model. The third column contains the types of statistics collected during the simulations. Slightly different statistics are collected for each type of element. The columns labeled 1 through 5 contain the statistics collected for each simulated 2-hour time period. Each number in the column labeled "Overall means" is the mean of the five numbers to its right.

For the first simulation, let's consider the element Door, which is an Entrance. We learn that 61 objects entered the model, whereas 13 were unable to enter the model. This means that during our first simulated two hours, 74 (= 61 + 13) objects arrived at the model, 61 of these entered Line, and 13 left the model because Line was full. As we noted above, these 13 objects did not return to the model during the simulation (if we wanted them to, then we would have to alter the model). The simulated *service level* is computed by SimQuick using the following formula:

$$\text{Service level} = \frac{\text{Objects entering process}}{\text{Objects entering process} + \text{Objects unable to enter}}$$

Or, in this case, for simulation 1:

$$\text{Service level} = \frac{61}{61 + 13} = .82$$

In words, the service level for each simulation is the fraction of demand that is satisfied.

Thus, a reasonable summary measure of the service level of the model would be the mean of the service levels for each simulation. This mean is also calculated by SimQuick and is provided in the column "Overall means"; in this case, it equals .89. In this example, it appears there is a large amount of variability in the service levels from the five simulations (it ranges from .82 to .98). Hence, we may want to increase the number of simulations to get a better estimate of the overall mean.

For the first simulation, let's next consider the element Line, which is a Buffer. First, we notice that 57 objects left the Line during the simulation and went to the Teller. We see that at the end of the simulated two hours there were 9 objects left in the Line. This makes sense because the Line started with 5 objects at the beginning of the simulation, 61 objects entered it, and 57 left, which leaves 9 objects at the end. You can also read the maximum, minimum, and mean number of objects in the Line during the simulation. Finally, we see that the "Mean cycle time" was 16.80. The *mean cycle time* of an object at a Buffer during a simulation is the mean number of time units during the simulation that an object spent in the Line. In terms of our model, this represents the mean waiting time of a person in line.

Next, let's consider the statistics collected for the element Teller, which is a Work Station:

"Final status" can be either Working or Not working, and simply describes what the Work Station is doing at the end of the simulation. "Final finished inventory" refers to a small internal buffer that Work Stations have. A Work Station has enough room to hold one object on which it has finished working (if it outputs more than one object per work cycle, then this number of objects is the capacity of this internal buffer). The Teller's finished inventory is always 0 because it can always pass finished objects to the Buffer called Served Customers. A Work Station will retain a finished object in its inventory when it cannot be passed to an output destination (e.g., a Buffer that is full or a Work Station that is working). If a Work Station has some finished inventory, then it cannot start working on a new object until this inventory drops to zero. Hence, a Work Station with some finished inventory is called *blocked*.

"Mean finished inventory" and "Mean cycle time (fin. inv.)" are statistics collected for the internal buffer and are analogous to the statistics we collect for Buffers. Note that "Mean cycle time (fin. inv.)" does not include the working time at the Work Station (it's equal to zero in all the simulations in this example).

"Work cycles started" indicates how many times the Work Station has begun working on an object, and "Fraction time working" indicates the fraction of the time of the entire simulation that the Work Station spent working (this is an important performance measure that is often called *utilization* in the context of machines in a factory). We see that the Teller is working constantly during simulations 1, 2, 4, and 5. However, the Teller is working 96% of the time during simulation 3. This means the Line must have been empty for a short amount of time during the third simulation, and we see that this is true because the "Minimum inventory" for the Line in simulation 3 is zero.

"Fraction time blocked" indicates the fraction of the time of the entire simulation that the Work Station was blocked. In the bank example, the Teller is never blocked.

Interpreting the results for the Buffer called Served Customers is the same as for the Line. Note that the "Mean cycle time" is "Infinity" because no objects ever leave this Buffer.

Observe that the results collected differ between the simulations because they are based on some randomly generated numbers.

In terms of these statistics, management is probably most interested in the "Overall mean cycle time" of the Line. This represents the mean amount of time a customer is waiting in line. It is defined as the mean of the "Mean cycle times" of the Line for each simulation. It is computed by SimQuick and reported in the fourth column of the Results sheet. In this example, the overall mean cycle time is 14.70 time units.

Another statistic, in which management might be interested, is the "Overall mean cycle time" of the Line plus the Teller. This represents the mean amount of time a customer is both waiting and being served. This is easy to compute from the Results using the following formula:

Overall mean cycle time of Line plus Teller =

Overall mean cycle time of Line + Overall mean working time of Teller

The overall mean working time of the teller is simply 2.2 time units (from Nor(2.2,.5)). Hence, the overall mean cycle time of the Line plus Teller equals 16.90 (= 14.70 + 2.2) time units.

Before using this model to experiment with changes in the process, management should make sure the results are close to what is observed in the real bank; this is called checking the *validity* of the model. The most important statistic to check in this case is probably the overall mean inventory or the overall mean cycle time of the Line. If the model is not valid, then the structure and statistical distributions in the model need to be checked against the real process. For example, suppose our model gives a good approximation to the real bank.

Improving the process, Variation 1

First, let's see how much the overall mean cycle time of the Line can be reduced by adding a second teller to our model. Here is our new process flow map:

Process Flow Map for Bank, Variation 1

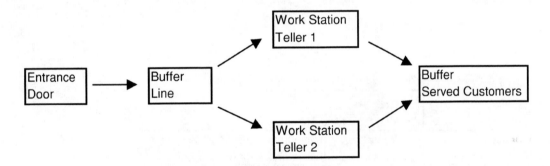

Assume both tellers can serve customers at the same rate. Can you guess by how much the overall mean inventory and the overall mean cycle time at Line will drop?

Here is the new SimQuick model:

Entrance:

1	
Name →	Door
Time between arrivals →	Exp(2)
Num. Objects per arrival →	1
Output Destination(s) ↓	
Line	

Buffers:

1			2	
Name →	Line		**Name** →	Served Customers
Capacity →	10		Capacity →	100
Initial # objects →	5		Initial # objects →	0
Output Destination(s) ↓	Output group size ↓		Output destination(s) ↓	Output group size ↓
Teller 1	1			
Teller 2	1			

Work Stations:

1			
Name →	Teller 1		
Working time →	Nor(2.2,.5)		
Output Destination(s) ↓	# of output objects ↓	Resource name(s) ↓	Resource # units needed ↓
Served Customers	1		

2			
Name →	Teller 2		
Working time →	Nor(2.2,.5)		
Output destination(s) ↓	# of output objects ↓	Resource name(s) ↓	Resource # units needed ↓
Served Customers	1		

Here are the results from running five simulations with SimQuick:

Simulation Results								
Element Types	**Element names**	**Statistics**	**Overall means**	**Simulation number(s)**				
				1	**2**	**3**	**4**	**5**
Entrance(s)	Door	Objects entering process	55.00	63	55	63	51	43
		Objects unable to enter	0.00	0	0	0	0	0
		Service level	1.00	1.00	1.00	1.00	1.00	1.00
Work Station(s)	Teller 1	Final status		Working	Working	Working	Working	Working
		Final finished inventory	0.00	0	0	0	0	0
		Mean finished inventory	0.00	0.00	0.00	0.00	0.00	0.00
		Mean cycle time (fin. inv.)	0.00	0.00	0.00	0.00	0.00	0.00
		Work cycles started	34.20	36	36	39	34	26
		Fraction time working	0.61	0.63	0.67	0.67	0.59	0.49
		Fraction time blocked	0.00	0.00	0.00	0.00	0.00	0.00
	Teller 2	Final status		Not Working	Not Working	Not Working	Working	Working
		Final finished inventory	0.00	0	0	0	0	0
		Mean finished inventory	0.00	0.00	0.00	0.00	0.00	0.00
		Mean cycle time (fin. inv.)	0.00	0.00	0.00	0.00	0.00	0.00
		Work cycles started	25.80	32	24	29	22	22
		Fraction time working	0.46	0.55	0.47	0.49	0.40	0.37
		Fraction time blocked	0.00	0.00	0.00	0.00	0.00	0.00
Buffer(s)	Line	Objects leaving	60.00	68	60	68	56	48
		Final inventory	0.00	0	0	0	0	0
		Minimum inventory	0.00	0	0	0	0	0
		Maximum inventory	5.00	5	5	5	5	5
		Mean inventory	0.28	0.25	0.36	0.37	0.23	0.19
		Mean cycle time	0.56	0.44	0.73	0.65	0.50	0.47
	Served Customers	Objects leaving	0.00	0	0	0	0	0
		Final inventory	58.60	67	59	67	54	46
		Minimum inventory	0.00	0	0	0	0	0
		Maximum inventory	58.60	67	59	67	54	46
		Mean inventory	30.76	32.98	31.74	34.70	28.32	26.04
		Mean cycle time		Infinite	Infinite	Infinite	Infinite	Infinite

The key statistic of interest is the overall mean cycle time for Line. The overall mean is now .56 time units. This is a clear improvement. We could use a t-test to prove that it is significant (see Appendix 1), but it is not necessary in this case. Also notice that the overall mean inventory of Line has significantly dropped to .28 objects. We see that the overall mean fraction time working of each teller (.61 and .46 time units) has dropped quite a bit. Finally, observe that the service level becomes 1 in each simulation. Hence, all our simulated customers were able to enter the bank.

Improving the process, Variation 2

Next, let's see if the waiting time can be reduced by adding an ATM to our model, instead of a second teller. Here is our new process flow map:

Process Flow Map for Bank, Variation 2

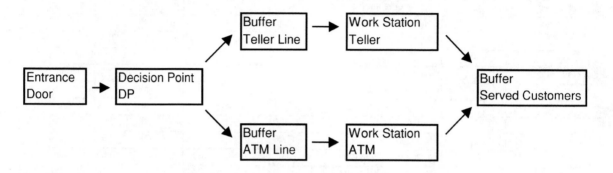

Note that this SimQuick model makes use of the Decision Point element. A Decision Point routes objects in one of two directions. When filling in a Decision Point table in SimQuick, we must specify a rule for determining in which direction each object goes. This rule is a probability, expressed in SimQuick as a percentage (i.e., a number between 0 and 100). Let's say we've done a bit of research (perhaps we've talked to or observed some similar banks that have this setup), and we estimate that approximately 20% of our customers will use an ATM located in the entrance hallway of our bank. Then, in our model, we specify that each object that enters the Decision Point goes to the Teller Line with an 80% probability and goes to the ATM Line with a 20% probability. (A Decision Point routes objects in zero time.)

Let's assume that the working time at an ATM has been observed to be a bit less than at a teller and that it can be approximated by a normal distribution with a mean of 1.5 minutes and a standard deviation of .3 minutes. Can you guess how the overall mean inventory and the overall mean cycle time at Teller Line will compare with the previous simulations?

Here is the new SimQuick model:

Entrance:

1	
Name →	Door
Time between arrivals →	Exp(2)
Num. objects per arrival →	1
Output destination(s) ↓	
DP	

Decision Point:

1	
Name →	DP
1st output destination →	Teller Line
1st output percent →	80
2nd output destination →	ATM Line
2nd output percent →	20

Buffers:

1		2	
Name →	Teller Line	**Name** →	ATM Line
Capacity →	10	Capacity →	3
Initial # objects →	4	Initial # objects →	1
Output destination(s) ↓	Output group size ↓	Output destination(s) ↓	Output group size ↓
Teller	1	ATM	1

3	
Name →	Served Customers
Capacity →	100
Initial # objects →	0
Output destination(s) ↓	Output group size ↓

Work Stations:

1			
Name →		Teller	
Working time →		Nor(2.2,.5)	
Output destination(s) ↓	# of output objects ↓	Resource name(s) ↓	Resource # units needed ↓
Served Customers	1		

2			
Name →		ATM	
Working time →		Nor(1.5,.3)	
Output Destination(s) ↓	# of output objects ↓	Resource name(s) ↓	Resource # units needed ↓
Served Customers	1		

Observe that the initial number of objects in the Teller Line has dropped from 5 to 4 and that the initial number of objects in the ATM Line is 1 (this reflects our 20–80% rule at the Decision Point).

Here are the results for five simulations:

Element types	Element names	Statistics	Overall means	Simulation number(s)				
				1	2	3	4	5
Entrance(s)	Door	Objects entering process	59.20	66	56	62	57	55
		Objects unable to enter	0.60	0	3	0	0	0
		Service level	0.99	1.00	0.95	1.00	1.00	1.00
Work Station(s)	Teller	Final status		Working	Working	Not Working	Working	Working
		Final finished inventory	0.00	0	0	0	0	0
		Mean finished inventory	0.00	0.00	0.00	0.00	0.00	0.00
		Mean cycle time (fin. inv.)	0.00	0.00	0.00	0.00	0.00	0.00
		Work cycles started	52.20	55	50	53	54	49
		Fraction time working	0.95	1.00	0.89	0.97	0.98	0.90
		Fraction time blocked	0.00	0.00	0.00	0.00	0.00	0.00
	ATM	Final status		Not Working	Not Working	Working	Not Working	Not Working

		Final finished inventory	0.00	0	0	0	0	0
		Mean finished inventory	0.00	0.00	0.00	0.00	0.00	0.00
		Mean cycle time (fin. inv.)	0.00	0.00	0.00	0.00	0.00	0.00
		Work cycles started	11.60	15	11	14	8	10
		Fraction time working	0.14	0.18	0.15	0.15	0.10	0.13
		Fraction time blocked	0.00	0.00	0.00	0.00	0.00	0.00
Buffer(s)	Teller Line	Objects leaving	52.20	55	50	53	54	49
		Final inventory	0.40	1	0	0	0	1
		Minimum inventory	0.00	0	0	0	0	0
		Maximum inventory	8.40	10	10	8	7	7
		Mean inventory	3.73	3.77	5.75	4.35	2.46	2.31
		Mean cycle time	8.61	8.23	13.80	9.86	5.47	5.67
	ATM Line	Objects leaving	11.60	15	11	14	8	10
		Final inventory	0.00	0	0	0	0	0
		Minimum inventory	0.00	0	0	0	0	0
		Maximum inventory	1.20	2	1	1	1	1
		Mean inventory	0.02	0.06	0.03	0.00	0.02	0.00
		Mean cycle time	0.23	0.52	0.34	0.02	0.25	0.00
	Served Customers	Objects leaving	0.00	0	0	0	0	0
		Final inventory	62.80	69	60	66	61	58
		Minimum inventory	0.00	0	0	0	0	0
		Maximum inventory	62.80	69	60	66	61	58
		Mean inventory	32.59	36.59	32.94	34.07	29.64	29.70
		Mean cycle time		Infinite	Infinite	Infinite	Infinite	Infinite
Decision Point(s)	DP	Objects leaving	59.20	66	56	62	57	55
		Final inventory	0.00	0	0	0	0	0

Let's consider the statistics collected for the Decision Point. We count the number of objects leaving it during each simulation and we also report "Final inventory," which is simply the number of objects at the Decision Point at the end of each simulation. A Decision Point can hold at most one object; hence, its "Final inventory" is 0 or 1. During a simulation, a Decision Point does not start routing a new object until its inventory is empty.

The key statistic of interest is the overall mean cycle time for both Teller Line and ATM Line. The overall mean for the Teller Line is now 8.61 time units. This is a clear improvement over the waiting time of the one-teller model. Again, we could use a t-test to prove that it is significant (see Appendix 1), but it appears to be unnecessary in this case. The overall mean for ATM Line is .23. Hence, customers electing to use the ATM would not have to wait long. Notice that the overall mean inventory of Teller Line has dropped to 3.73, also a clear improvement over our one-teller model. Finally, note that the overall mean service level is .99, not quite 1 as in our two-teller model, but an apparent improvement over the one-teller model.

So what should management do? Both improvement ideas should reduce the waiting time, although the two-teller idea appears to be significantly more effective than the ATM idea. So now the decision comes down to costs and what kind of service the bank wants to offer its customers.

Exercise 1: For each of the following models, run 20 simulations.

a. Consider the original, one-teller, bank process described in Example 1, except assume the working time for each teller is approximated by a normal distribution with a mean of 3 minutes and a standard deviation of .5 minutes. Report the overall mean cycle times in the Line when there are one, two, and three tellers.

b. Consider the ATM variation in Example 1 (with the original working times provided in the example). We assumed a 20% probability that each customer would use the ATM. Report the overall mean cycle times in the Teller Line when this probability is set at 15%, 20%, 25%, and 30%. This is an example of *sensitivity analysis*, where certain estimated inputs to a model are varied to see what effect this has on the results of the simulations.

Section 2: Additional waiting line processes

In this section, we examine a variety of waiting line processes. Some of these models are more complex than the bank example in that they contain more SimQuick elements and, more important, they contain more sources of uncertainty. When the number of statistical distributions and/or the amount of variability in the statistical distributions of a model increases, it's likely there will be more variation in the statistics that are collected. To compensate for this, it may be necessary to increase the number of simulations so the overall means of the data that are collected tend to be more consistent from one batch of runs to another. An alternative, if this makes sense for the problem under consideration, is to increase the number of time units per simulation.

Example 2: A grocery store checkout

Consider a grocery store between the hours of 5 P.M. and 8 P.M. on a weeknight. Suppose three checkout lanes are typically open, each checkout can handle customers with any number of items, and each checkout has a dedicated bagger. It has been observed that checking out (including bagging) takes a mean of 3 minutes per customer and that this is approximately normally distributed with a standard deviation of .5 minutes. The mean amount of time between customer arrivals at the checkouts is 1 minute and can be approximated by an exponential distribution. Although customers initially enter one specific line, they will move to a different line if it looks faster.

Hint: Model the three lines as a single line that feeds all the checkouts. You can assume that everyone that arrives at the checkout gets into the line, regardless of its length; thus, no one is rejected from the process. (So make sure your single line is large enough.)

Exercise 2:

a. Draw a process flow map for your three-lane model.

For parts b to d, perform 20 simulations for each. Assume there is no one in line at the beginning of the simulations.

b. Run the model from part a and report, for (the single) line, the overall mean number of customers and the overall mean waiting time.

c. How much would the overall mean number of customers and the overall mean waiting time in (the single) line be reduced by opening a fourth checkout?

d. The owner of the grocery store chain is considering the purchase of new bar code scanners. This would reduce the mean checkout time to 2.6 minutes (still normal), with a standard deviation of .5 minutes. For the three-lane case, what effect would this have on the overall mean number of customers and the overall mean waiting time in (the single) line?

e. Suppose approximately 25% of the customers purchase 10 items or less. Management is considering adding one special checkout lane for these people. Modify your process flow map from part a for this situation (you need not perform any simulations).

Example 3: A fast-food restaurant drive-thru

Management wants to study the drive-thrus at a number of Burger Queen (BQ) restaurants during the peak hours of 11 A.M. to 2 P.M. The process works as follows. Cars arrive and line up to place an order. It's been observed that the time between car arrivals can be approximated by an exponential distribution with a mean of 2.3 minutes. There is only room for five cars to line up. The time to place an order is also roughly exponentially distributed and takes a mean of 2 minutes per car. Cars then move forward to a single window at which they pay and pick up their order. Two cars can fit between a car placing an order and another car at the pay/pick-up window. The amount of time a car sits at the pay/pick-up window can be approximated by an exponential distribution with a mean of 2.2 minutes.

Exercise 3: For each of the following parts, perform 20 simulations. Assume that at 11 A.M. there is typically one car in line to place an order and one car in line to pay/pick up their order. For a process flow map of this process, see the left side of the process flow map for Example 7.

a. Build a SimQuick model of the drive-thru, as described. Report the overall mean throughput (i.e., the overall mean <u>final</u> inventory in Served Cars). Also report the overall mean cycle time for the whole process. This number is the mean amount of time an object spends between entering the Buffer called Outside Order Line and leaving the Work Station called Pay/Pickup. It can be obtained by adding the overall mean cycle time through the two Buffers, the mean working time at the two Work Stations (obtained from their input distributions), and the overall mean cycle time through the internal buffer at the Work Station called Car Order. Also report the overall mean service level of the customers arriving at the process.

b. The BQ design team is thinking about installing a faster process for making hamburgers. They believe this could reduce the time for Pay/Pickup to a mean of 1.5 minutes, again exponentially distributed. What effect would this have on the numbers reported in part a?

Example 4: A call center

A process flow map for a call center is provided on the following page. Here's how this process works. Customers with questions about this company's products call an 800 number. During a typical 8-hour day shift, the time between calls can be approximated by an exponential distribution with a mean of 2.5 minutes. If the call center is not too busy, a machine answers the call. One of two things can now happen, depending on a quick decision by the caller: Either the call is routed to another machine or a customer support (CS) person. There is about a 30% chance that any given call is routed to the machine. The call center machine can handle two calls at the same time and have two calls on hold (one in Machine Line and one in the Decision Point's internal buffer). The service time of each machine-handled call can be approximated by a normal distribution, with a mean of 4.5 minutes and a standard deviation of 1.2 minutes. The service time of each human-handled call can be approximated by a normal distribution, with a mean of 12 minutes and a standard deviation of 1 minute. The call center has 10 phone lines and hence can handle up to 10 calls at once.

Note: The Decision Point has an internal buffer capacity of 1 and the Buffer called Machine Line has a capacity of 1. Because there are only 10 phone lines, the number of CS people plus the capacity of the CS Line must be 6.

Process Flow Map for Call Center

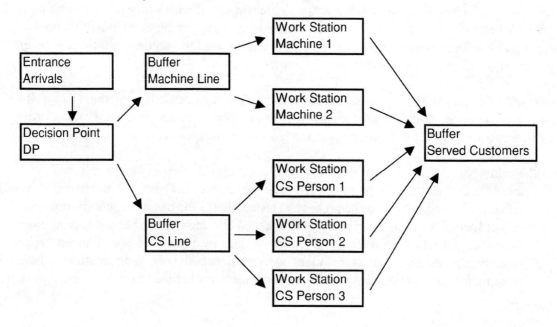

Exercise 4: Management wants to determine how many CS people to use so that the mean number of minutes a person waits is less than 2 minutes and so that the service level is at least .9. Consider using from one to five CS people. For each possibility, run 20 simulations of an 8-hour day shift and record the mean cycle time through the Machine Line and the CS Line (assume the Buffers are initially empty). How many CS people would you recommend?

Example 5: A Department of Motor Vehicles

A process flow map for a Department of Motor Vehicles (DMV) in a small town is provided on the following page. Here is how the process works: During the peak demand hours of 10 A.M. to 1 P.M., customers arrive, one at a time, at the DMV every 4 minutes (on average, according to an exponential distribution). Each customer gets into a line (with a capacity of 10 people). After waiting in line, each customer discusses what they need with a clerk. Typically, 20% of the customers want to register their car (only), 40% want to renew their licenses (only), and 40% want to do both. Those who want to do both get their license renewed first. The time of this discussion can be approximated by a normal distribution with a mean of 1 minute and a standard deviation of .1 minutes. The clerk gives each customer a number and shows them where to sit (there is plenty of room for customers to sit and wait). Observe that the Decision Point called Choice 1 separates the customers into those that only want to register their car and the rest. A second Decision Point called Choice 2 is used to separate the people who only want a license from the people who want a license and a registration. (Be careful in setting the probabilities for these Decision Points.) The amount of time for a clerk to process a license renewal can be approximated by a normal distribution with a mean of 5 minutes and a standard deviation of .5 minutes. The amount of time for a clerk to process a registration can be approximated by a normal distribution with a mean of 6 minutes and a standard deviation of .5 minutes.

Process Flow Map for DMV

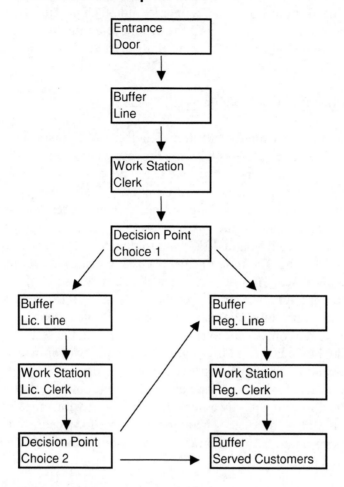

Exercise 5: Management is considering adding a new license clerk. They want to know the effect of this on the following statistic: the overall mean waiting time in the process of those customers that need both a license and a registration (i.e., the sum of the overall mean cycle times in the three lines plus the mean working times of all three types of clerks). Perform 30 simulations of the present situation (for the 3-hour time period) and the situation with a new license clerk. (We perform more simulations in this case because there are more sources of uncertainty in this model.) Report the above statistic for both cases. Also report the overall mean cycle time in both the license and registration lines in each case. Can you explain the change in the cycle times in the individual lines? Assume there are no people in the lines at the beginning of the simulations.

Section 3: Advanced waiting line processes

In this section, we make use of two advanced features of SimQuick called *resources* and *priorities*. They will allow us to model more complex waiting line processes. Resources are defined and assigned to Work Stations in the SimQuick tables. The basic idea is that a Work Station cannot start working on an object unless it has all the resources that have been assigned to it. If several

Work Stations use the same resource, and if this resource is in limited supply, then a Work Station may not be able to start working, even though it has input objects and is not presently working. When two Work Stations are competing for a limited resource, the Work Station with higher priority gets it. The priority of a Work Station is determined by the number of the table in SimQuick into which it has been entered (the lower the number, the higher the priority). The details are provided in the following two examples that involve a fast-food restaurant.

Example 6: Value meals at a fast-food restaurant

Customers at a Burger Queen fast-food restaurant can buy food in two basic ways: a value meal or a la carte. There are five choices of value meals; each choice includes a sandwich, an order of fries, and a medium drink. The restaurant encourages customers to buy value meals by pricing them below what the same order would cost a la carte. The value meal concept results in two benefits for the restaurant. First, it simplifies their inventory by reducing demand variability, which results in lower inventory costs. Second, it tends to take less time to deliver a value meal order to a customer than an a la carte order. It's this second benefit that we examine in this example.

Currently, this restaurant has two servers during the peak hours of 5 P.M. to 7 P.M. Given the present selection of value meals and their pricing, 30% of the customers during these hours choose value meals. The amount of time for a server to prepare a value meal can be approximated by a normal distribution, with a mean of 1.2 minutes and a standard deviation of .1 minutes. The amount of time for a server to prepare an a la carte meal can be approximated by a normal distribution, with a mean of 2.5 minutes and a standard deviation of .5 minutes. (We assume customers are served one at a time and the time to pay for an order is included in the preparation time.) The time between arrivals of individual customers at the restaurant can be approximated by an exponential distribution with a mean of .8 minutes. There is room for about 15 customers to stand in line. A process flow map is provided below.

Process Flow Map for Value Meals at a Fast-food Restaurant

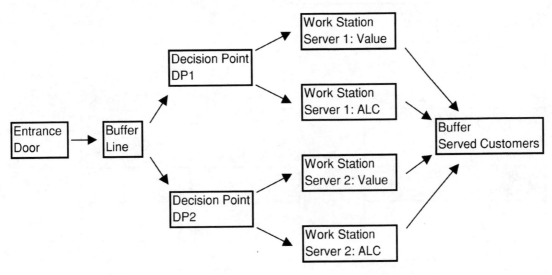

In this model, each server is modeled by two Work Stations. For example, Server 1: Value models the preparation of a value meal order by Server 1 and Server 1: ALC models the preparation of an a la carte order by Server 1. Thus, the working times of these two Work Stations are different. Because a server can only fill one order at a time, we can only allow one of these two Work Stations to work at a time. This is accomplished in SimQuick by using an advanced feature called *resources*. The idea is to assign a common resource, say R1, to Server 1: Value and Server 1: ALC. Then one of these Work Stations can work only if it has this resource. We do the same thing with a different resource for Server 2: Value and Server 2: ALC. Next, we address the details.

When using resources, we must inform SimQuick how many of each we have available. To do this, click on the "Resources" button on the Control Panel and fill in the table as follows.

Resources:

Name ↓	Number available ↓
R1	1
R2	1

Here are the remaining SimQuick tables to be filled in.

Entrance:

1	
Name →	Door
Time between arrivals →	Exp(.8)
Num. objects per arrival →	1
Output destination(s) ↓	
Line	

Buffers:

1			**2**		
Name →	Line		**Name** →	Served Customers	
Capacity →	15		Capacity →	500	
Initial # objects →	5		Initial # objects →	0	
Output destination(s) ↓	Output group size ↓		Output destination(s) ↓	Output group size ↓	
DP1	1				
DP2	1				

Work Stations:

1

Name →	Server 1: Value		
Working time →	Nor(1.2,.1)		
Output destination(s) ↓	# of output objects ↓	Resource name(s) ↓	Resource # units needed ↓
Served Customers	1	R1	1

2

Name →	Server 1: ALC		
Working time →	Nor(2.5,.5)		
Output destination(s) ↓	# of output objects ↓	Resource name(s) ↓	Resource # units needed ↓
Served Customers	1	R1	1

3

Name →	Server 2: Value		
Working time →	Nor(1.2,.1)		
Output destination(s) ↓	# of output objects ↓	Resource name(s) ↓	Resource # units needed ↓
Served Customers	1	R2	1

4

Name →	Server 2: ALC		
Working time →	Nor(2.5,.5)		
Output destination(s) ↓	# of output objects ↓	Resource name(s) ↓	Resource # units needed ↓
Served Customers	1	R2	1

Decision Points:

1

Name →	DP1
1st output destination →	Server 1: Value
1st output percent →	30
2nd output destination →	Server 1: ALC
2nd output percent →	70

2

Name →	DP2
1st output destination →	Server 2: Value
1st output percent →	30
2nd output destination →	Server 2: ALC
2nd output percent →	70

In general, in order to work, a Work Station must acquire the prescribed number of each resource that has been assigned to it. Once a Work Station has acquired a resource, it retains that resource until it's finished working. At that time, the resource becomes available to any Work Station that requires it. In this example, each Work Station requires one unit of its resource and there is only one unit of each resource available; thus, only one Work Station of each pair can work at a time. Therefore, in this example, the resource goes to the Work Station that has an input. These inputs are determined by the Decision Points according to the demand for each type of meal. Thus, DP1 sends 30% of its objects to Server 1: Value and DP2 sends 30% of its objects to Server 2: Value.

Exercise 6: Management wants to study the effect of the pricing of value meals on the waiting time of customers. They are considering pricing schemes that would effectively set demand for value meals at 30%, 35%, and 40% of total demand. Run 20 simulations of a Burger Queen (BQ) restaurant for each of these schemes and report the overall mean waiting time in line of the simulated customers.

Example 7: Cross-trained workers at a fast-food restaurant

Consider the BQ restaurant described in Exercise 3, part b (you don't need to work Exercise 3 in order to do Exercise 7 below). The BQ design team is considering the possibility of cross-training the worker assigned to the pay/pick-up window, whose working time at Pay/Pickup can be approximated by an exponential distribution with a mean of 1.5 minutes. Thus, if no one is at the pay/pick-up window, this person would serve a walk-in customer. The process flow map is provided below.

Process Flow Map for a Cross-trained Worker at a Fast-food Restaurant

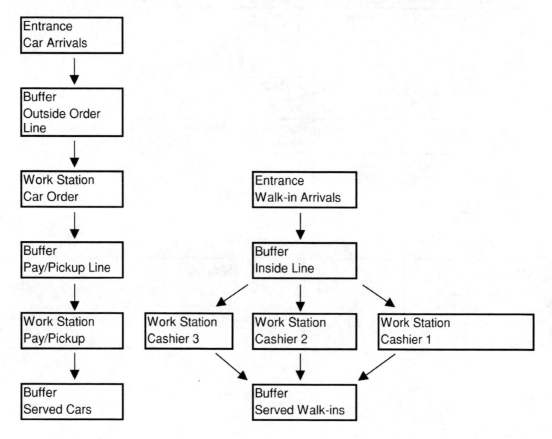

Note that this process has two Entrances, one for cars at the drive-thru and one for people entering the restaurant. We want this process to work in the usual fashion except that only one (cross-trained) person is operating both Work Stations Pay/Pickup and Cashier 3. In particular, if there is a customer in the Pay/Pickup Line, then the cross-trained person should serve this customer next. However, if there is no customer in the Pay/Pickup Line, if both Cashier 1 and Cashier 2 are serving customers, and if there is a customer in the Inside Line, then the cross-trained person should serve this customer at the Work Station called Cashier 3. (Of course, once the cross-trained person starts serving an inside customer, he or she should finish serving this customer before going back to serve a drive-thru customer that may have arrived at the window.)

Here are the additional details for this example: The time between the arrivals of walk-ins can be approximated by an exponential distribution with a mean of 2 minutes. The Inside Line can hold about 15 people. The amount of time for a cashier to serve a customer can be approximated by a normal distribution with a mean of 4.1 minutes and a standard deviation of .5 minutes. The details for the drive-thru are the same as for Exercise 3, part b.

This situation can be modeled with SimQuick using *resources* and *priorities*. To implement this, simply fill in the SimQuick tables as usual, except for the following:

Click on the "Resources" button on the Control Panel and fill in the table as follows:

Name ↓	Number available ↓
CT Worker	1

CT Worker represents our cross-trained worker and 1 means we have one such resource available. Next we assign this resource to the two Work Stations that need it to work: Pay/Pickup and Cashier 3. The Work Station tables are filled in as follows:

2			
Name →	Pay/Pickup		
Working time →	Exp(1.5)		
Output destination(s) ↓	# of output objects ↓	Resource name(s) ↓	Resource # units needed ↓
Served Cars	1	CT Worker	1

	5		
	Name →	Cashier 3	
	Working time →	Nor(4.1,.5)	
Output destination(s) ↓	# of output objects ↓	Resource name(s) ↓	Resource # units needed ↓
Served Walk-ins	1	CT Worker	1

The 1 under "Resource # units needed" means that Pay/Pickup and Cashier 3 need one unit of CT Worker to work. Because we have only 1 such unit available, only one of these two Work Stations can work at once.

The final issue is priority. This is determined by the number of the table into which the Work Stations have been entered. For this example, Cashiers 1 and 2 have priority over Cashier 3 (i.e., they will take customers from Inside Line before Cashier 3 does). Also, Pay/Pickup has priority over Cashier 3: If CT Worker is not working and there are customers in both Pay/Pickup Line and Inside Line, then CT Worker will go to Pay/Pickup and serve the drive-thru customer. Thus, we have entered Cashiers 1, 2, and 3 into Work Station tables 3, 4, and 5, respectively, and we have entered Pay/Pickup into Work Station table 2. (Car Order is in table 1.)

Exercise 7:

a. Run 20 simulations of the model assuming there is no cross-trained worker (i.e., there is no Work Station called Cashier 3 and there is no cross-trained worker; hence, there is a worker exclusively working at Pay/Pickup and it's not necessary to use any resources). Report the overall mean cycle time in the Inside Line, the overall mean cycle time for the whole drive-thru process (this is defined in Exercise 3), the service levels both inside and outside, and the fraction time working of Pay/Pickup.

b. Run 20 simulations of the model with the cross-trained worker. Report the same numbers as in part a. Also report the "mean number in use" for the resource CT Worker (this can be found at the bottom of the Results page). This represents the fraction of time the cross-trained worker is working and should be equal to the sum of the fraction time working of Pay/Pickup and Cashier 3.

Chapter 3: Inventory and Supply Chains

Learning objectives:

- To model, simulate, and analyze two widely used inventory systems: "order-up-to" and reorder point
- To model, simulate, and analyze a supply chain
- To understand the following performance measures: service level, ordering costs, and holding costs
- To understand the trade-offs between: order size, reorder point, service level, lead time, ordering costs, and holding costs
- To understand the SimQuick element Exits

Overview

In this chapter, we address the basic question of inventory management: How much and when to order? We do this first from the viewpoint of a store and then from the viewpoint of a warehouse that supplies a number of stores. Finally, we combine these two viewpoints and consider the basic question for a supply chain.

We look at two simple and widely used inventory policies: the "order-up-to" and the "reorder point" system (these are defined in the examples). A key performance measure in each example is the *service level* of the customer (i.e., the fraction of demand that is satisfied). Another key performance measure (except in the first example) is *inventory cost*: *ordering cost* plus *holding cost*. With the reorder point system, we illustrate the fundamental trade-off between these two costs. (The ordering cost is the cost to place an order; it is considered to be independent of the size of the order and hence consists mainly of the cost of preparing an order, but may also include, for example, transportation costs. The holding cost is the cost of holding one item in inventory for some period of time; a major component of the holding cost is the cost of having money, which could be invested elsewhere, tied up in inventory.)

A new SimQuick element called an Exit is introduced in this chapter. The details are covered in Example 8. Exits are used to model customer demand and are quite similar to the Entrances, which were introduced in the previous chapter.

Inventory problems of the type we consider are often addressed using standard formulas. An advantage of using process simulation to address inventory problems is that you are not limited to the assumptions underlying the formulas. In particular, with simulation, you have more freedom in describing the statistical properties and the detailed workings of the process (this can be seen in Examples 10 and 11). A disadvantage of using simulation for inventory problems (and for "optimization" problems, in general) is that you may have to perform a large number of simulations to find a solution; and this solution is not guaranteed to be optimal.

The exercises in this section require the reader to run a basic model multiple times with only small changes. Using some simple features of Excel can ease this work. This is described for Example 8 in Appendix 1 under "Multiple SimQuick runs."

The sections in this chapter build on one another and should be read in sequence.

Section 1: An "order-up-to" inventory policy

Example 8: Grocery store inventory

Management at a grocery store has received some complaints from customers that the store occasionally runs out of SuperWheat bread, which is baked by the SuperBread Company. Here is how the inventory process presently works.

A truck from the SuperBread bakery drops off several types of loaves of freshly baked bread at the grocery store every other day. For each type of bread from the bakery, there is designated space on the shelves of the store and in the back of the store (the total space allotted to each type of bread depends on the demand for that type of bread). The driver drops off enough loaves of each type so the designated space for each type of bread is filled. (This is a simple version of what is sometimes referred to as an *order-up-to* inventory policy.) The store has designated enough space to hold 70 loaves of SuperWheat bread. An examination of sales records (on days when the store doesn't run out of SuperWheat) shows that the daily demand for SuperWheat is uncertain but has a mean of 40 loaves. The store is open 12 hours per day, 7 days per week.

Management wants to determine the amount of storage space that should be designated for SuperWheat bread so that 99% of the customer demand is satisfied. Management is also curious to know, on average, how long a loaf of SuperWheat bread is in the store.

Modeling the process with SimQuick

This process can be modeled with three elements. A process flow map and the three SimQuick tables are provided below. For this model, time units represent hours that the store is open and objects represent loaves of SuperWheat.

Process Flow Map for Grocery Store Inventory

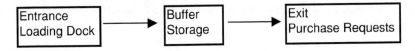

Entrance:

1	
Name →	Loading Dock
Time between arrivals →	24
Num. objects per arrival →	200
Output destination(s) ↓	
Storage	

Buffer:

1	
Name →	Storage
Capacity →	70
Initial # objects →	0
Output destination(s) ↓	Output group size ↓
Purchase Requests	1

Exit:

1	
Name →	Purchase Requests
Time between departures →	Exp(.3)
Num. objects per departure →	1

The arrivals of SuperWheat at the store are modeled by an Entrance with the name Loading Dock. The "Time between arrivals" is 24, which is the number of hours in two working days at the store. The "Number of objects per arrival" is 200, which is an arbitrary large number; it simply means the delivery truck carries lots of bread and can easily supply the store with as much bread as needed on each delivery.

The storage space for SuperWheat at the store (space on the shelf plus space in the back of the store) is modeled by a Buffer with the name Storage. When a shipment of objects (loaves) arrives, as much as will fit is moved into this Buffer (objects in the shipment that don't fit are simply taken away and cannot return at a later time (who wants old bread?)).

Loaves are removed from store inventory when a customer makes a "purchase request" and there is a loaf in inventory. Purchase requests are modeled by an Exit called Purchase Requests. Note that for an Exit we must specify the "Time between departures." In our model, this represents the time between purchase requests. We have observed that a mean of 40 purchases are made each day; hence, the mean time between purchase requests is (12 hours)/(40 purchases) = .3 hours per purchase request. As with the bank example, the distribution of time between arrivals of people at services is typically exponential, thus we have entered Exp(.3) for "Time between departures." The "Number of objects per departure" is 1 (the typical number of loaves sold at a time; if there was more uncertainty here, we could enter one of our statistical distributions). If during the simulation a purchase request occurs, but there is no object in Storage, then this is a lost sale (also called a *stockout*). SimQuick will keep track of these. (In general, if the "Num. of objects per departure" is bigger than 1, then this number of objects (or as many as are available) is removed from the process.)

Management estimates that this demand pattern should be the same for the next 30 working days, so let's set the "Time units per simulation" to be 360 (= (30 days) * (12 hours/day)) and let's run five simulations.

Interpreting SimQuick results

Here is what happened during one set of five runs.

Simulation Results								
Element types	**Element names**	**Statistics**	**Overall means**	**Simulation number(s)**				
				1	**2**	**3**	**4**	**5**
Entrance(s)	Loading Dock	Objects entering process	1038.20	1029	1046	1039	1033	1044
		Objects unable to enter	1961.80	1971	1954	1961	1967	1956
		Service level	0.35	0.34	0.35	0.35	0.34	0.35
Buffer(s)	Storage	Objects leaving	1037.60	1029	1046	1037	1033	1043
		Final inventory	0.60	0	0	2	0	1
		Minimum inventory	0.00	0	0	0	0	0
		Maximum inventory	70.00	70	70	70	70	70
		Mean inventory	30.82	30.93	29.81	32.08	31.17	30.12
		Mean cycle time	10.70	10.82	10.26	11.14	10.86	10.40
Exit(s)	Purchase Requests	Objects leaving process	1037.60	1029	1046	1037	1033	1043
		Object departures missed	161.00	186	192	113	157	157
		Service level	0.87	0.85	0.84	0.90	0.87	0.87

Let's consider the results for the Exit: Purchase Requests. In the first simulation, the number 1029 refers to the number of simulated loaves purchased. The number 186 refers to the number of simulated purchase requests that were not filled (i.e., the number of lost sales). Hence, for each simulation, the total demand during the 30 simulated days is given by

$$\text{Objects leaving process} + \text{Object departures missed}$$

The *service level* for each simulation is defined to be the fraction of demand that is satisfied; it is calculated as follows:

$$\text{Service level} = \frac{\text{Objects leaving process}}{\text{Objects leaving process} + \text{Object departures missed}}$$

Hence, for the first simulation,

$$\text{Service level} = \frac{1029}{1029 + 186} = .85$$

A reasonable measure of the service level of the process is the overall mean of the service levels calculated for each simulation. This is also calculated by SimQuick in the fourth column. In this example, it is equal to .87.

Note that the overall mean cycle time at Storage gives us an estimate of how long loaves of SuperWheat sit in inventory at the store before being purchased (in this case, 10.70 hours of working time).

Exercise 8:

a.   Vary the "Capacity" of Storage from 70 to 94 in increments of 4. For each capacity level, perform 20 simulations and report the overall mean service level for Purchase Requests. (Recall that we assume the bakery has adequate capacity to supply these various amounts to the store because we have set "Number of objects per arrival" to 200.) Also report the overall mean cycle time of simulated loaves in Storage. What level of inventory do you recommend to achieve a service level of .99?

b.   Store management is considering having the bakery make deliveries every day instead of every other day. This will allow the store to reduce the shelf space dedicated to SuperWheat (and other products from this bakery) and thereby offer some additional products to the customers. For this scenario, vary the "Capacity" of Storage from 34 to 54 in increments of 4. For each capacity level, perform 20 simulations and report the overall mean service level for Purchase Requests. Also report the overall mean cycle time of simulated loaves in Storage. What level of inventory do you recommend to achieve a service level of .99?

Section 2: A reorder point inventory policy

In this section, we illustrate the reorder point inventory policy by considering two examples: an electronics superstore and a warehouse.

Example 9: An electronics superstore

A large electronics superstore sells a popular handheld computer. The store presently manages its inventory of this item with the following process: When the number of computers in stock drops to 20, it places an order for 35 to the manufacturer. (20 is called the *reorder point* and 35 is called the *order size*.) The amount of time to receive an order varies a bit, but can be approximated by a normal distribution with a mean of 5 days and a standard deviation of .3 days. By looking at sales figures for days when the store does not run out of computers, management observes that the mean demand is 5 computers per day (the store is open 10 hours per day, 7 days per week). The store estimates that during the next 2 months this demand pattern should remain steady.

Management wants to satisfy at least 90% of the customer demand directly from the store's inventory. Subject to this, of course, management wants to minimize its costs. In this case, the costs are $100 every time an order is placed (regardless of its size) and $.50 per day for every computer that is in inventory at the store. Management wants to determine whether it should change its reorder point and order size.

Modeling the process with SimQuick

The inventory process used by this store can be modeled in SimQuick using four elements. A process flow map and the SimQuick tables are provided below. For this model, time units represent hours and, of course, objects represent computers.

Process Flow Map for an Electronics Superstore

Buffers:

1			2	
Name →	Factory		**Name** →	Reorder Point
Capacity →	1000		Capacity →	20
Initial # objects →	1000		Initial # objects →	20
Output destination(s) ↓	Output group size ↓		Output destination(s) ↓	Output group size ↓
Delivery	35		Purchase Requests	1

Work Station:

1				
	Name →	Delivery		
	Working time →	Nor(50,3)		
Output destination(s) ↓	# of output objects ↓	Resource name(s) ↓	Resource # units needed ↓	
Reorder Point	35			

Exit:

Name →	Purchase Requests
Time between departures →	Exp(2)
Num. objects per departure →	1

The Exit called Purchase Requests models customer demand. Requests for this product occur, on average, five times per day hence the mean time between requests is 2 hours (=10 hours/5 purchases per day). Making the standard assumption of an exponential distribution, we enter Exp(2) for the "Time between departures" of the Exit. We assume computers are typically purchased one at a time and enter 1 for the "Number of objects per departure."

Store inventory is modeled by objects in two locations in our SimQuick model: the Buffer called Reorder Point and the internal buffer of the Work Station called Delivery.

Recall: Every Work Station has an internal buffer that can hold the objects completed after one working cycle (called *finished inventory*). As long as there are objects in this buffer, the Work Station cannot start working on a new object and it is called *blocked*.

As this model runs, the Exit pulls objects from Reorder Point, and Reorder Point pulls objects from the internal buffer of Delivery. Consider what happens when the number of objects in the internal buffer hits zero. At this time, the inventory in our simulated store is entirely contained in the Reorder Point Buffer; hence, the amount of inventory is less than or equal to the reorder point of 20 (which is the capacity of Reorder Point). Also, at this time, Delivery becomes unblocked and pulls an object from Factory and begins working on it. This corresponds to placing an order. Note that the working time of Delivery is the delivery time from the factory: Nor(50,3) because there are 10 working hours per day. When Delivery finishes working, it deposits 35 objects into its internal buffer (35 is the "Number of output objects" for Delivery, which is the order size). As many of these objects as possible are passed to Reorder Point, where they become available to our simulated customers. Delivery is blocked until it can pass all its inventory to Reorder Point (at which point another simulated order is placed).

Note that the "Output group size" of the Buffer called Factory is equal to 35. This means that every time Delivery obtains one object from Factory, the number of objects in Factory drops by 35. Also note that the "Initial # objects" of the Buffer called Reorder Point is 20. Thus, each simulation begins with the placement of an order.

Because the demand pattern is expected to remain stable for two months, the number of time units per simulation should be 600 (= (2 months)*(30 days per month)*(10 hours per day)).

Below is the output from five simulations of the present inventory policy.

Simulation Results

Element types	Element names	Statistics	Overall means	Simulation number(s) 1	2	3	4	5
Work Station(s)	Delivery	Final status		Working	Working	Working	Working	Working
		Final finished inventory	0.00	0	0	0	0	0
		Mean finished inventory	2.97	3.37	3.39	2.71	2.68	2.71
		Mean cycle time (fin. inv.)	7.27	8.24	8.29	6.64	6.55	6.64
		Work cycles started	8.00	8	8	8	8	8
		Fraction time working	0.65	0.60	0.63	0.66	0.66	0.68
		Fraction time blocked	0.35	0.40	0.37	0.34	0.34	0.32
Buffer(s)	Factory	Objects leaving	280.00	280	280	280	280	280
		Final inventory	720.00	720	720	720	720	720
		Minimum inventory	720.00	720	720	720	720	720
		Maximum inventory	1000.00	1000	1000	1000	1000	1000
		Mean inventory	853.41	858.89	858.25	853.02	848.12	848.74
		Mean cycle time	1828.73	1840.48	1839.11	1827.90	1817.40	1818.74
	Reorder Point	Objects leaving	260.80	248	261	265	265	265
		Final inventory	4.20	17	4	0	0	0
		Minimum inventory	0.00	0	0	0	0	0
		Maximum inventory	20.00	20	20	20	20	20
		Mean inventory	12.45	12.78	13.19	11.92	12.53	11.83
		Mean cycle time	28.68	30.93	30.32	27.00	28.36	26.80
Exit(s)	Purchase Requests	Objects leaving process	260.80	248	261	265	265	265
		Object departures missed	46.40	57	25	48	46	56
		Service level	0.85	0.81	0.91	0.85	0.85	0.83

Observe that the overall mean service level of .85 is below management's goal of satisfying 90% of the customer demand. Service level is most directly affected by the reorder point in the inventory policy. Hence, it appears that the present reorder point of 20 must be increased.

Next, let's consider how to calculate the cost of this inventory policy. First, the store pays $100 for every order it places. The mean number of orders placed in our simulations is the overall mean number of Work cycles started at the Work Station called Delivery (8 in this case). Hence, we may estimate the store's ordering costs during the simulations to be ($100 per order)*(8 orders) = $800. The store also pays $.50 per day for every computer that is in inventory at the store. The overall mean number of computers in inventory is the sum of the overall mean number in the internal buffer of Delivery plus the overall mean number in ROP. Hence, we may estimate the store's holding costs during the simulations to be (60 days)*($.50 per day per computer)*(2.97 + 12.45 computers) = $462.60. So the total costs are $800.00 + $462.60 = $1262.60.

Finally, it's easy to estimate the overall mean amount of time that a computer sits in inventory at the store. It's given by the overall mean cycle time of the internal buffer of Delivery plus the overall mean cycle time of ROP. In this case, we get $7.27 + 28.68 = 35.95$ hours.

Management has decided to consider a number of different scenarios in looking for a solution to their inventory problem. These scenarios are summarized by the rows in the following table.

Order Size	Reorder Point
35	25
45	25
55	25
65	25
75	25

Exercise 9: For each scenario in the previous table, run 20 simulations and report the overall mean service level and the estimated total cost. Does this new reorder point achieve the desired service level of .9? If so, which scenario would you recommend? As the order size increases, what happens to the ordering and holding costs?

Example 10: A warehouse

A warehouse temporarily holds printers for a chain of computer stores. Trucks from the stores arrive periodically to pick up printers. Exactly when pick-ups occur and how many printers are picked up is uncertain because it depends on the demand at the stores. The time between the arrival of each truck can be approximated by an exponential distribution with a mean of 2 days. The number of printers that are requested at each pick-up can be approximated by a normal distribution with a mean of 12 and a standard deviation of 1. The time to receive an order from the factory can be approximated by a normal distribution with a mean of 7 days and a standard deviation of 1 day. The warehouse wants to satisfy at least 90% of the demand from the stores. The warehouse is considering the reorder point scenarios (rows) in the following table.

Order Size	Reorder Point
80	50
120	50
160	50
200	50
80	60
120	60
160	60
200	60

Exercise 10:

a.   The warehouse estimates that it costs them $.25 per day for every printer held in inventory and it costs $300 for every order placed to the factory (regardless of the order size). The warehouse estimates that demand should remain about the same for the next 200 days (time units in SimQuick should represent days). For each scenario, run 20 simulations and report the overall mean service level and the estimated total cost. Which scenario would you recommend?

Hint: For the Exit in the model, you must enter statistical distributions for both "Time between departures" and "Num. objects per departure."

b.   The warehouse is considering using a different company to transport printers from the factory. It is estimated that the delivery time for this company could be estimated by a normal distribution with a mean of 4 days and a standard deviation of 1 day; however, the fixed cost per order would increase to $500. The warehouse believes this will allow them to significantly lower their reorder point, but will probably require them to increase their order size. For each scenario (row) in the following table, run 20 simulations and report the overall mean service level and the estimated total cost. Would you recommend switching delivery companies and, if so, which scenario would you recommend?

Order Size	Reorder Point
80	20
120	20
160	20
200	20
240	20

Section 3: A Supply Chain Process

Let's build on the electronics superstore example and the warehouse example from the previous section, by considering them simultaneously in a supply chain. In this example, two electronics stores order from a regional warehouse. The same company owns the stores and the warehouse. The warehouse orders from a factory, which is owned by a different company. Thus, the store management now has control of two levels of the supply chain. The key question is still: How much and when to order? However, management now must consider inventory that occurs in several places of the process, including the delivery trucks!

Example 11: Two stores and a warehouse

Consider a company that manages two electronics stores that sell the same popular handheld computer. Orders are placed to a regional warehouse, also owned by this company. The regional warehouse places orders to the manufacturer (which is not owned by the company). The amount of time to receive an order at either store can be approximated by a normal distribution with a mean of 1 day and a standard deviation of .1 days. The amount of time to receive an order at the warehouse can be approximated by a normal distribution, with a mean of 4 days and a standard deviation of .2 days. The mean demand for this computer at each store is five computers per day (both stores are open 10 hours per day, 7 days per week). The demand is expected to remain the same at both stores for the next 60 days.

Management wants to use a reorder point scheme at the stores and the warehouse. Their goal is to achieve at least a 95% service level at each store at minimum cost. The ordering costs are $75 every time a store places an order to the warehouse and $150 every time the warehouse places an order to the factory. It also costs $.50 per day for every computer in inventory at a store, and $.10 per day for every computer in inventory at the warehouse. We assume it also costs $.10 per day for every computer in transit from the warehouse to a store.

Modeling the process with SimQuick

A process flow map follows.

Process Flow Map for a Supply Chain

```
                    ┌─────────────────────┐
                    │ Buffer              │
                    │ Factory             │
                    └─────────────────────┘
                               │
                               ▼
                    ┌─────────────────────┐
                    │ Work Station        │
                    │ Delivery to Warehouse│
                    └─────────────────────┘
                               │
                               ▼
                    ┌─────────────────────┐
                    │ Buffer              │
                    │ Warehouse ROP       │
                    └─────────────────────┘
                      ╱                 ╲
                     ▼                   ▼
      ┌─────────────────────┐   ┌─────────────────────┐
      │ Work Station        │   │ Work Station        │
      │ Delivery to Store 1 │   │ Delivery to Store 2 │
      └─────────────────────┘   └─────────────────────┘
                 │                          │
                 ▼                          ▼
      ┌─────────────────────┐   ┌─────────────────────┐
      │ Buffer              │   │ Buffer              │
      │ Store 1 ROP         │   │ Store 2 ROP         │
      └─────────────────────┘   └─────────────────────┘
                 │                          │
                 ▼                          ▼
      ┌─────────────────────┐   ┌─────────────────────┐
      │ Exit                │   │ Exit                │
      │ Store 1 Pur. Req.   │   │ Store 2 Pur. Req.   │
      └─────────────────────┘   └─────────────────────┘
```

Let time units in SimQuick represent hours. Thus, the delivery time to the stores from the warehouse is modeled by Nor(10,1) and the delivery time to the warehouse from the factory is modeled by Nor(40,2).

Finally, let's consider how to calculate the cost of inventory in transit from the warehouse to the store. To begin, we calculate the mean inventory in transit to Store 1 (this is done similarly for Store 2):

$$\begin{pmatrix} \text{Mean in - transit} \\ \text{inventory to Store 1} \end{pmatrix} = \begin{pmatrix} \text{Overall mean of} \\ \text{"fraction of time working"} \\ \text{at Delivery to Store 1} \end{pmatrix} * (\text{Order size to Store 1})$$

We now get the following approximation:

The total cost of in-transit inventory (during the simulation) =

$$\left[\begin{pmatrix} \text{Mean in - transit} \\ \text{inventory to Store 1} \end{pmatrix} + \begin{pmatrix} \text{Mean in - transit} \\ \text{inventory to Store 2} \end{pmatrix} \right] * (\$.50 \text{ per computer per day}) * (60 \text{ days})$$

Note that 60 days is the number of simulated days.

Exercise 11: Build the SimQuick model for the supply chain. For each scenario (row) in the following table, run 20 simulations and report the mean of the overall mean service levels for the two stores and the estimated total cost. Which scenario should management adopt?

Warehouse ord. size	Warehouse ROP	Store ord. size	Store ROP
100	50	40	10
100	50	45	10
100	50	50	10
200	50	40	10
200	50	45	10
200	50	50	10

Note: The times at which objects move in the supply chain model are determined by the inventory levels in various Buffers. This is a key element in many *just-in-time* (JIT) processes where shipment departures are triggered by inventory levels in such a way that shipments tend to arrive just before inventory runs out. Example 12 in Chapter 4 illustrates how this strategy works within a single facility.

Chapter 4: Manufacturing

Learning objectives:

- To model, simulate, and analyze the following types of processes: linear flow, cellular, assembly/disassembly, batch, and job shop
- To model and analyze the following features of a process: quality testing and machine breakdowns
- To understand the following performance measures: throughput, cycle time, mean inventory level, service level, utilization, flow time, and tardiness
- To understand the following concepts: bottleneck, setup, and batch size
- To understand the following priority rules: shortest processing time and nearest due date
- To understand the trade-offs between working time variability, inventory level, and throughput; number of workers and throughput; and batch size and service level
- To understand the advanced SimQuick features of resources and priorities

Overview

In this chapter, we discuss a variety of process types typically associated with manufacturing. We consider processes where products are made in a line, where products are split apart and reassembled, where products are made in batches, and where many different products may go through the same machine (a job shop). We also consider processes where something can go wrong in either the form of a quality problem with a product or a reliability problem with a machine.

In most cases, the performance measure that most interests us is the *capacity* of the process; that is, we want to study the maximum amount that can be produced during some time period. This is also sometimes called the *throughput* of the process. Thus, we do not explicitly incorporate customer demand into most of these models (although it can easily be added). In the batch process example, customer demand is included in the model and service level becomes a key performance measure. In the job shop example, we are interested in two different performance measures: the average production time (i.e., the mean cycle time or mean *flow time* or mean *lead time*) and the on-time performance (in particular, the mean *tardiness*). These measures will be defined in the examples.

In the linear flow process, we examine the trade-offs between working time variability, inventory level, and throughput. In the cellular manufacturing process, we examine the trade-off between the number of workers and the throughput. In the assembly/disassembly process, we examine how to identify a bottleneck (by considering *utilization*) and the effect on throughput of reducing the bottleneck. In the batch process example, the concepts of *batch size* and *setups* are introduced and the trade-off between batch size and service level are examined.

In general, the processes considered in this chapter are parts of larger processes. Thus, the models in this chapter may be thought of as building blocks for more complex processes. In fact, the processes in this chapter may be combined with the inventory and supply chain processes from the previous chapter to model even more complex processes.

The job shop, quality, and reliability processes make use of the advanced SimQuick features called *resources* and *priorities*.

Section 1: Linear flow processes

By a linear flow process, we mean a process that can be modeled as a series of Buffers and Work Stations, possibly with an Entrance at one end and an Exit at the other end. Hence, objects are passed from one element to the next as capacity, demand, and supply dictate. Processes of this type are common in factories. Examples include the manufacturing of home appliances, computer equipment, and automobiles.

The first example we consider is a generic small model. What makes this model interesting is the variation in the working times at the Work Stations. As the exercise demonstrates, this variation plays an important role in the performance of the process.

In the second example, we consider a special type of linear flow process called a *cell*. In this type of process, the work stations are very close together. This has two effects: The amount of inventory is typically low and workers can operate more than one machine. In this example, we consider the performance of the process with various numbers of workers.

Example 12: A generic linear flow process

In this example, we consider a simple process described by the following process flow map:

Process Flow Map for a Linear Flow Process

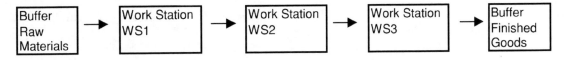

We let time units denote minutes. The working time at each Work Station is uncertain, but can be approximated the same way: by a uniform distribution with minimum of 5 minutes and maximum of 15 minutes (i.e., enter Uni(5,15) for the working times). Hence, the line is *balanced* in the sense that the mean working time at each Work Station is the same (however, there is a lot of variance in the working times). We run the model for a simulated 24-hour time period, that is, 1440 time units. For the capacity and initial inventory of Raw Materials, enter 200 (this will prevent us from running out). Also enter 200 for the capacity of Finished Goods (its initial inventory should be 0).

We could easily make the model more realistic by incorporating an Entrance for the raw materials and an Exit for the finished goods (this would allow us to model arrivals and departures from the process due to, say, trucking schedules). In fact, this is done in Appendix 2. By keeping things simple for now, we can examine, in the exercise, some key relationships involving the following: inventory (between the Work Stations), variability (in working times), and throughput (the number of finished goods produced per 8-hour shift).

Due to the variability in working times, the following situation is likely to occur when you run this model in SimQuick: WS2 finishes working on an object, while WS3 is still working on another object. When this happens, WS2 puts its finished object into its internal buffer, which can hold only one object in this model. Until this object has been passed to WS3, WS2 cannot start working on a new object. WS2 is said to be *blocked* while it is waiting for WS3 to finish. You can learn what fraction of the entire simulation WS2 is blocked by looking on the Results sheet under "Fraction time blocked" for WS2.

Exercise 12: For each of the situations a through e below, perform 20 simulations and report the overall mean throughput (i.e., the overall mean <u>finished</u> inventory of Buffer: Finished Goods).

a.   Consider the SimQuick model described above. Note that the "Working time" for each Work Station is Uni(5,15).

b.   Consider the original model, changing the working time at each Work Station to Uni(9,11). Note that the new working times have the same mean but a smaller variance.

c.   Consider the original model, using the reduced variance distribution from part b on WS2 only.

d.   For the original model, add a Buffer between WS1 and WS2 and another Buffer between WS2 and WS3. Report the overall mean throughput when the capacity of both Buffers is set to 1, then 3, then 5, then 7, and then 9. As you increase the Buffer capacity, does the throughput improve over what you reported in part a?

e.   Consider the model in d (with the Buffer capacities at 9), using the reduced variance distributions from b.

f.   Summarize your results from parts a through e. In particular, discuss the relationship between inventory, working time variability, and throughput.

Note: In our model, we have limited the amount of inventory allowed between Work Stations and these limits control the way objects flow through the process. In a real process, an inventory limit between work stations is sometimes enforced with *kanbans* (a simple system typically involving the use of cards). This is a key component in many JIT processes.

Example 13: A Manufacturing Cell

For this example, we consider a linear flow process where the work stations are close together and hence there is little room for inventory between stations. When a process of this type consists of machines arranged in a "U-shape" in a factory, it is often called a *cell*. The reason for a U-shaped configuration is to make it more convenient for each worker to operate two or more machines. In this example, we are interested in the effect on throughput of using 6 vs. 3 vs. 2 workers in this cell. We assume here that when a machine is running, it must be attended by a worker (hence, a worker cannot start a machine working on a part and then go do something else while it's working). We consider a process with the following flow map.

Process Flow Map for Cellular Manufacturing

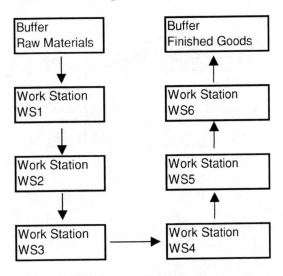

As in Example 12, time units represent minutes and we assume that the working time at each Work Station can be approximated by a uniform distribution with minimum value 5 and maximum value 15. If we enter this model as usual into SimQuick, then we are modeling the situation where each machine has its own dedicated worker.

Next, we consider the case of running the cell with three workers. (The case with two workers is left to the reader.) Let's say that Worker 1 is assigned to WS1 and WS2, Worker 2 is assigned to WS3 and WS4, and Worker 3 is assigned to WS5 and WS6. These workers are modeled in SimQuick as *resources*. When using resources in SimQuick, we must inform SimQuick how many of each we have available. To do this, click the "Resources" button on the Control Panel. Fill in the table as follows:

Name ↓	Number available ↓
Worker 1	1
Worker 2	1
Worker 3	1

In this case, we have only one of each worker available. However, a resource could represent a group of people (e.g., maintenance workers) or a set of identical tools, in which case there could be more than one available.

Click on "Return to Control Panel" followed by "Work Stations." Fill in tables 1 and 2 as follows (note how we are assigning the resource Worker 1 to WS1 and WS2):

1			
Name →	WS1		
Working time →	Uni(5,15)		
Output destination(s) ↓	# of output objects ↓	Resource name(s) ↓	Resource # units needed ↓
WS2	1	Worker 1	1

2			
Name →	WS2		
Working time →	Uni(5,15)		
Output destination(s) ↓	# of output objects ↓	Resource name(s) ↓	Resource # units needed ↓
WS3	1	Worker 1	1

Similarly, fill in the tables for WS3 and WS4 with Worker 2 and fill in the tables for WS5 and WS6 with Worker 3.

Here is what happens when SimQuick runs. If a Work Station is not working, if it contains no finished object in its internal buffer, if there is an input object available, and if the resource it requires is available, then it takes the input object and the resource and begins working. The resource then becomes unavailable to other Work Stations. When a Work Station finishes working on an object, it makes the resource available to other Work Stations. This means that, in this model, each Worker will alternate between his or her two machines, working on one object each time.

Observe that when a model with resources is run, the Results sheet reports the "Mean number in use" for each Resource.

Exercise 13: Run 20 simulations for each of the situations described above: with six, three, and two workers (for the two-worker case, assign one worker to WS1, WS2, and WS3 and assign the other worker to the other Work Stations). Run each simulation for 1440 time units (i.e., 24 simulated hours). Make sure you set the capacity and initial number of objects for Raw Materials and the capacity of Finished Goods to be sufficiently large (200 will do the job). Report the overall mean throughput for each case (i.e., the overall mean <u>finished</u> inventory in

Finished Goods). Also report the overall mean throughput divided by the number of workers for each situation. Which situation has the best throughput per worker?

Section 2: Assembly/disassembly processes

In this section, we consider two common activities in a process: taking several different parts and combining them into one part (assembly), and taking one part and breaking it into several different parts (disassembly). This is easy to model with SimQuick.

Example 14: Box manufacturing

Here we describe a (simplified) process for making wooden jewelry boxes. Each box is made from the following parts: two identical square pieces (the top and bottom), four identical rectangular pieces (the sides), and a hinge. At the beginning of the process is a pile of sheets of wood. One sheet at a time is taken to a machine, called Cutter. From each sheet, this machine cuts out four square pieces and eight rectangular pieces. (Note that the Cutter produces enough for two boxes due to the size of the sheets.) The four square pieces are then sent to a buffer, followed by a machine, called TB Finishing, for making them into tops and bottoms, followed by another buffer. The eight rectangular pieces are also sent to a buffer, followed by a machine, called S Finishing, for making them into sides, followed by another buffer. A Work Station, called Box Assembly, then takes a top, a bottom, and four sides and constructs boxes, one at a time. Further details are provided below.

Management believes the machine S Finishing is a *bottleneck*. This means they believe that, if this machine were replaced with a faster machine, the number of boxes produced each day (i.e., the *throughput*) would increase. In particular, management wants to know how much the throughput would increase if the machine were replaced with a new machine whose working time can be approximated by a normal distribution with a mean of 2.5 minutes and a standard deviation of .5 minutes.

Modeling the process with SimQuick

The following process flow map describes the present process:

Process Flow Map for Box Manufacturing

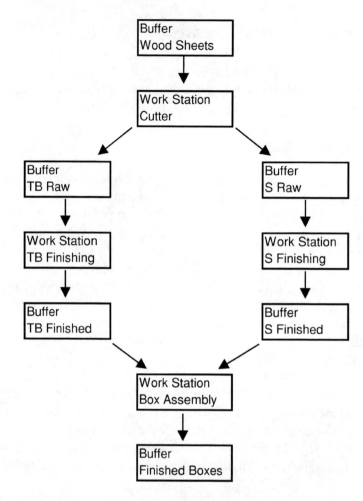

Next, we present the SimQuick model. Time units represent minutes. Note that for the Work Stations we have added statistical distributions that approximate the "real" working times and for the Buffers we have added capacities and estimates of typical initial inventory levels.

Work Stations:

		1	
	Name →	Cutter	
	Working time →	Nor(10,1)	
Output destination(s) ↓	# of output objects ↓	Resource name(s) ↓	Resource # units needed ↓
TB Raw	4		
S Raw	8		

2			
Name →	TB Finishing		
Working time →	Nor(5,1)		
Output destination(s) ↓	# of output objects ↓	Resource name(s) ↓	Resource # units needed ↓
TB Finished	1		

3			
Name →	S Finishing		
Working time →	Nor(4,1)		
Output destination(s) ↓	# of output objects ↓	Resource name(s) ↓	Resource # units needed ↓
S Finished	1		

4			
Name →	Box Assembly		
Working time →	Nor(10,2)		
Output destination(s) ↓	# of output objects ↓	Resource name(s) ↓	Resource # units needed ↓
Finished Boxes	1		

Buffers:

1	
Name →	Wood Sheets

1	
Name →	Wood Sheets
Capacity →	100
Initial # objects →	100
Output Destination(s) ↓	Output group size ↓
Cutter	1

2	
Name →	TB Raw

2	
Name →	TB Raw
Capacity →	10
Initial # objects →	2
Output destination(s) ↓	Output group size ↓
TB Finishing	1

3	
Name →	S Raw
Capacity →	20
Initial # objects →	20
Output destination(s) ↓	Output group size ↓
S Finishing	1

4	
Name →	TB Finished
Capacity →	10
Initial # objects →	8
Output destination(s) ↓	Output group size ↓
Box Assembly	2

5	
Name →	S Finished
Capacity →	20
Initial # objects →	0
Output destination(s) ↓	Output group size ↓
Box Assembly	4

6	
Name →	Finished Boxes
Capacity →	500
Initial # objects →	0
Output destination(s) ↓	Output group size ↓

Let's consider the Work Station called Cutter. First, observe that it has one input, the Buffer called Wood Sheets. Hence, this Work Station takes one object at a time from Wood Sheets and works on it. However, this Work Station has two outputs: TB Raw and S Raw, with "# of output objects" of 4 and 8, respectively. Hence, after finishing a work cycle, this Work Station sends 4 objects to TB Raw and 8 objects to S Raw (i.e., it takes 1 object in and sends 12 objects out). In general, a Work Station with two or more outputs can be said to be performing a *disassembly* (in addition to splitting materials into pieces, multiple outputs can be used to model, for example, the disassembly of a machine at a maintenance center).

These objects then work their way through the Work Stations called TB Finishing and S Finishing, one at a time. Next observe that the Buffers called TB Finished and S Finished have "Output group sizes" of 2 and 4, respectively. This means that objects leave these Buffers 2 and 4 at a time, respectively, and that these groups of 2 and 4 are each considered to be a single object.

Finally, let's consider the Work Station called Box Assembly. It has two inputs. When a Work Station has more than one input, it cannot start a work cycle until it has one of each type of input. In this case, this means that the Box Assembly cannot start working until there are at least 2 objects in TB Finished (which are considered as a single object for output to Box Assembly) and 4 objects in S Finished (which are considered as a single object for output to Box Assembly). When one of each input object is available, a Work Station takes them and starts working. Thus, multiple inputs into a Work Station can be used to model an *assembly* operation.

Note 1: A Work Station can have both multiple inputs and multiple outputs.

Note 2: Multiple inputs and outputs can also be used to model "signaling," where a Work Station sends a message to another Work Station to begin working (see Example 15).

Exercise 14: Perform 20 simulations with the SimQuick model of the existing process and report the throughput (i.e., the overall mean number of boxes produced during 8 working hours). Also report the overall mean fraction time working (also called *utilization*) for each Work Station Which Work Station is a *bottleneck* according to this statistic (i.e., has highest value)? Rerun the simulations with the new Work Station and report the same statistics. Is there a significant improvement in throughput? Is the work more evenly balanced between the Work Stations (i.e., the overall mean fraction time working)?

Section 3: Batch and job shop processes

In this section, we consider two important types of processes. Both are fairly complex in that they involve special rules that create new modeling challenges. Batch processes are used, for example, in the manufacturing of food, clothing, and pharmaceuticals. Batch processes typically have a machine that is used to manufacture several different products. It is time consuming and expensive to switch the machine from making one product to another (such a switch is called a *setup*). Thus, each product is made in fairly large batches. The result is that inventory can pile up. Hence, an important question: How large should these batches be so that demand is satisfied and inventory does not pile up too much? We consider this question in Example 15.

Job shop processes are used, for example, in the manufacturing of machine parts, in the maintenance of jet engines, and for the care of patients in a hospital. Job shops typically have a variety of work stations and can make a variety of different products. With so many different types of jobs moving through a job shop at a time, an important question becomes the following: In what order should jobs be processed at each machine? We consider this question in Example 16.

Example 15: Pharmaceutical manufacturing

A pharmaceutical company makes a number of products in pill form. Two such products, Aspirin A and Aspirin B, have a high and steady demand and a single machine has been dedicated to making them. This machine can only make one type of pill at a time and must be thoroughly cleaned (i.e., *setup*) when it switches from making one type of pill to another. Management must decide how much of each type of pill to make at a time to satisfy 90% of the demand for each product; in operations lingo, management must decide on the best *batch sizes*.

Let us simplify the process as follows. First, assume we have as much raw material (chemicals in powder form) as we need. (Once we design the rest of the process, we can arrange with our supplier to deliver the quantities we need, when we need them.) The raw materials can be grouped into batches of anywhere from 100 to 500 lbs (in increments of 100 lbs). Batches are sent to the machine that creates the pills (pills are created by applying enormous pressure to the chemicals placed into pill-shaped molds). Every time the machine finishes a batch, it must be washed out before a batch of the other product can be started. The setup times are normally distributed with a mean of 3 working hours and a standard deviation of .5 hours. Actual processing times for a batch are the same for each product and are provided in the following table.

	Batch Sizes (lbs.)				
	100	200	300	400	500
Processing Times (hr)	Nor(1,.5)	Nor(2,.6)	Nor(3,.7)	Nor(4,.8)	Nor(5,.9)

After processing, the pills go into a storage area with a very large capacity. Pills are removed from the storage area as demand dictates: The time between shipments for Aspirin A is exponentially distributed with a mean of 20 working hours and each shipment is 300 lbs (or as much as is available); the time between shipments for Aspirin B is exponentially distributed with a mean of 10 working hours and each shipment is 300 lbs (or as much as is available).

Management is considering the following scenarios, or combinations of batch sizes.

	Scenarios (batch sizes in lbs)					
	1	**2**	**3**	**4**	**5**	**6**
Aspirin A	100	100	200	300	300	400
Aspirin B	200	300	300	400	500	500

For example, under scenario 1, 100 lbs of Aspirin A followed by 200 lbs of Aspirin B are made on the machine, then the pattern is repeated. Management wants to know how much finished inventory and what service level would result from each scenario.

Modeling the process with SimQuick

A process flow map and SimQuick model (for scenario 6) follow. Each object corresponds to 100 lbs of materials (either raw materials or finished pills). Time units correspond to hours.

Process Flow Map for a Batch Process

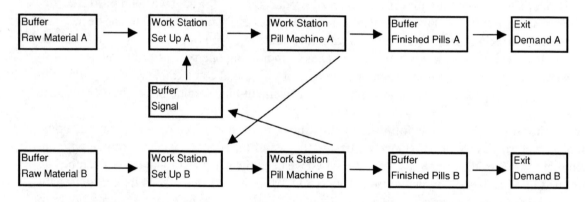

Buffers:

1	
Name →	Raw Material A
Capacity →	500
Initial # objects →	500
Output destination(s) ↓	Output group size ↓
Set Up A	4

2	
Name →	Finished Pills A
Capacity →	500
Initial # objects →	10
Output destination(s) ↓	Output group size ↓
Demand A	1

3	
Name →	Raw Material B
Capacity →	500
Initial # objects →	500
Output destination(s) ↓	Output group size ↓
Set Up B	5

4	
Name →	Finished Pills B
Capacity →	500
Initial # objects →	10
Output destination(s) ↓	Output group size ↓
Demand B	1

5	
Name →	Signal
Capacity →	1
Initial # objects →	1
Output destination(s) ↓	Output group size ↓
Set Up A	1

Work Stations:

1			
Name →	Set Up A		
Working time →	Nor(3,.5)		
Output destination(s) ↓	# of output objects ↓	Resource name(s) ↓	Resource # units needed ↓
Pill Machine A	1		

2			
Name →	Pill Machine A		
Working time →	Nor(4,.8)		
Output destination(s) ↓	# of output objects ↓	Resource name(s) ↓	Resource # units needed ↓
Finished Pills A	4		
Set Up B	1		

3		
Name →	Set Up B	
Working time →	Nor(3,.5)	

Output destination(s) ↓	# of output objects ↓	Resource name(s) ↓	Resource # units needed ↓
Pill Machine B	1		

4		
Name →	Pill Machine B	
Working time →	Nor(5,.9)	

Output destination(s) ↓	# of output objects ↓	Resource name(s) ↓	Resource # units needed ↓
Finished Pills B	5		
Signal	1		

Exits:

1	
Name →	Demand A
Time between departures →	Exp(20)
Num. objects per departure →	3

2	
Name →	Demand B
Time between departures →	Exp(10)
Num. objects per departure →	3

Let's consider how this model works. The real pill machine is modeled by the four Work Stations in this model. Each Work Station corresponds to one of the activities that can take place at the real pill machine: setups for Aspirin A and B and production of Aspirin A and B. Hence, in the model we will have only one of these four Work Stations in operation at a time.

A Work Station in SimQuick can begin working if it has one of each of its input objects and no finished inventory (in its internal buffer). When this model is started, no Work Station has any finished inventory and only Set Up A has each of its inputs (the one object in Signal and an object from Raw Material A). Hence, the model begins with Set Up A, taking these two objects and performing a simulated setup of the pill machine for making Aspirin A. Note that the "Output group size" of Raw Material A is 4. This means that the number of objects in Raw Material A drops by four when one object is removed (this corresponds to 400 lbs of chemicals, which is the batch size for this scenario). When this setup is complete, Pill Machine A is the only Work Station with all its inputs; hence, it begins to process this batch. The Working time is taken from the previous table. When Pill Machine A finishes working, it outputs four objects to Finished Pills A (the batch is broken back into its 100-lb components for departures) and one object to Set Up B. The object sent to Set Up B is a signal that Pill Machine A is done. With this signal, Set Up B now has both its input objects and can begin working. Note that when it takes one object from Raw Material B, the number of objects in Raw Material B drops by five.

When this setup is complete, Pill Machine B begins to process a batch (again, the time is taken from the table above). When Pill Machine B finishes working, it outputs five objects to Finished Pills B (the batch is again broken up for departures). It also outputs 1 object to Signal, thus allowing the cycle to repeat.

Finally, during the simulation, pills leave the system from the two Exits according to the demand for each product. Note that we start the simulation with typical amounts of finished pills of each type.

Exercise 15: Simulate this process for 10 weeks (assume there are 8 working hours per day and 5 working days per week). Perform 20 simulations for each scenario. For each scenario, report the overall mean number of setups (this is given by the sum of the overall mean number of "Cycles started" at Set Up A and Set Up B), the overall mean inventory in each of the two finished pill storage areas, and the overall mean service level for each product. Discuss how you would decide which batch size to use.

Example 16: A single-machine job shop

For this example, we build a model of a single machine in a job shop. The model can easily be extended to include multiple machines (up to the limitations of SimQuick). For example, in a factory, the machine could be a lathe, a drill, or a saw or, in a service operation, it could represent an insurance claim check or a mortgage credit check.

The machine in this example processes four types of jobs. Arrivals of jobs are uncertain as are the processing times. They can be approximated by the SimQuick distributions in the following table (time units represent working hours; there are eight working hours per day). Processing times include the time for setting up the machine. Because each job is actually a batch, the processing times can be fairly long for some jobs. Once a job is started at the machine, it is finished before another job is started. The table also contains the lead time (number of hours between the arrival of the job and when it is finished) that is quoted to customers for each type of job.

Job	Time between arrivals	Processing time at machine	Quoted lead time
Job 1	Nor(13,3)	Nor(7,1)	16
Job 2	Nor(28,3)	Nor(8,1)	36
Job 3	Nor(32,3)	Nor(4,1)	24
Job 4	Nor(24,3)	Nor(3,1)	8

Management wants to compare two *priority rules* (which are used for deciding which job to do next at the machine):

<u>Shortest Processing Time</u>: When the machine finishes work on a job, it works next on the job that has the smallest (mean) processing time among the jobs that are ready to go.

<u>Nearest Due Date</u>: When the machine finishes work on a job, it works next on the job that has the smallest lead time among the jobs that are ready to go.

Modeling the process with SimQuick

A process flow map is provided below.

Process Flow Map for a Single-machine Job Shop

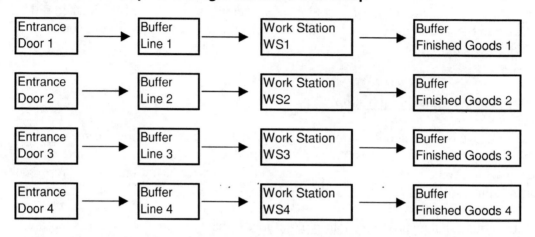

The model works as follows. Jobs of type 1 arrive at Door 1, jobs of type 2 arrive at Door 2, and so on. Hence, the "Time between arrivals" at each Entrance is the distribution given for the corresponding job type. After a job arrives, it goes into a Buffer for its type. The machine is modeled by the four Work Stations. The "Working time" of each Work Station is the processing time given for the corresponding job type. Of course, when we run the model, we want only one Work Station to be working at a time. To accomplish this, we assign a common resource, say R1, to each Work Station and make only one unit of this resource available. A Work Station must have this resource to work and, because there is only one unit available, only one Work Station can work at a time. When a Work Station finishes working on an object, the resource becomes available. It is taken by the highest *priority* Work Station that has an input object ready to go. The priority of a Work Station is simply determined by the number of its SimQuick table. For example, suppose during a simulation that the Work Station in table 1 finishes working on an object. If there is an input object for this Work Station, then it keeps the resource and begins working on that object. Suppose there is no such object. If the Work Station in table 2 has an input object, it acquires the resource and begins working on that object, and so on. Thus, to model the shortest processing time rule, we fill in the Work Station tables of SimQuick in the order WS4, WS3, WS1, WS2.

The Work Station tables for the shortest processing time model are provided below. Also provided is the Resource table (click on the "Resources" button on the Control Panel). It must be filled in so SimQuick knows how much of each resource is available. (If we changed the 1 in this table to a 2, then two of the Work Stations in our model could work at the same time.)

Work Stations:

1

Name →	WS4	
Working time →	Nor(3,1)	
Output destination(s) ↓	# of output objects ↓	Resource name(s) ↓	Resource # units needed ↓
Finished Goods 4	1	R1	1

2

Name →	WS3	
Working time →	Nor(4,1)	
Output destination(s) ↓	# of output objects ↓	Resource name(s) ↓	Resource # units needed ↓
Finished Goods 3	1	R1	1

3

Name →	WS1	
Working time →	Nor(7,1)	
Output destination(s) ↓	# of output objects ↓	Resource name(s) ↓	Resource # units needed ↓
Finished Goods 1	1	R1	1

4

Name →	WS2	
Working time →	Nor(8,1)	
Output destination(s) ↓	# of output objects ↓	Resource name(s) ↓	Resource # units needed ↓
Finished Goods 2	1	R1	1

Resources:

Name ↓	Number available ↓
R1	1

Finally, we need to discuss how management decides between the two different priority rules. We consider two performance measures for comparing the priority rules; they are expressed in terms of *flow time*. The *mean flow time of a job type* is the mean amount of time that type of job spends waiting plus being processed. The *tardiness of a job type* is zero if its mean flow time is less than or equal to its quoted lead time and

(the mean flow time of the job type) – (the quoted lead time),

otherwise.

Management is interested in two performance measures:

The *overall mean flow time* is the mean of the mean flow times of each job type.

The *overall tardiness* is the mean of the tardinesses of each job type.

Exercise 16: For the job shop described above, run 30 simulations with each priority rule. Make sure the capacity of each Finished Goods Buffer is large enough (100 will do the job). Management assumes that the demand patterns should remain stable for the next 100 days. For each rule, report the overall mean flow time and the overall tardiness.

Section 4: Quality and reliability in processes

In this section, we consider how to model two things in a factory that can go wrong. The first process involves quality problems with a product, and the second process involves reliability problems with a machine.

Example 17: A quality control station

Let's consider a simple process with a quality control station. Suppose we have an ample supply of raw materials, in this case, printed circuit boards. These boards are passed, one at a time, to a work station where a worker installs a few components. Each board is then passed to a quality control station where the installation is tested. Ninety percent of the boards pass this test and are then put into finished goods inventory. Those that fail the test are returned to the worker to be immediately examined and then retested. Management wants to know if investing in a new machine for the component installation would improve the throughput of the process. The new machine would have the same working time as the old machine, but the number of boards that pass inspection should increase to 95%. The remaining details are provided below.

Modeling the process with SimQuick

Here is a process flow map.

Process Flow Map for a Quality Control Station

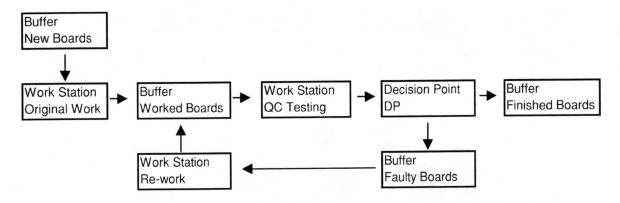

Observe that Original Work and Re-work are done at the same location in the factory by the same person. Hence, only one of these can be done at a time, so we assign a common resource to them. We also want Re-work to have a higher *priority* than Original Work. This means that if both Work Stations are ready to start working at some point in the simulation, then Re-work gets the resource and starts working first. We instruct SimQuick to do this by entering Re-work into a table with a smaller number than Original Work. Hence, we have put Re-work into table 2 and Original Work into table 3, below. The effect of this is that whenever there is rework to be done, it is done before any new work is started. Here is how the SimQuick model looks (time units represent minutes).

Buffers:

1	
Name →	New Boards
Capacity →	200
Initial # objects →	200
Output destination(s) ↓	Output group size ↓
Original Work	1

2	
Name →	Worked Boards
Capacity →	20
Initial # objects →	0
Output destination(s) ↓	Output group size ↓
QC Testing	1

3	
Name →	Faulty Boards
Capacity →	20
Initial # objects →	0
Output destination(s) ↓	Output group size ↓
Re-work	1

4	
Name →	Finished Boards
Capacity →	200
Initial # objects →	0
Output destination(s) ↓	Output group size ↓

Work Stations:

1			
Name →	QC Testing		
Working time →	Nor(3,.5)		
Output destination(s) ↓	# of output objects ↓	Resource name(s) ↓	Resource # units needed ↓
DP	1		

2			
Name →	Re-work		
Working time →	Nor(8,1)		
Output destination(s) ↓	# of output objects ↓	Resource name(s) ↓	Resource # units needed ↓
Worked Boards	1	R1	1

3			
Name →	Original Work		
Working time →	Nor(5,1)		
Output destination(s) ↓	# of output objects ↓	Resource name(s) ↓	Resource # units needed ↓
Worked Boards	1	R1	1

Decision Point:

1	
Name →	DP
1st output destination →	Finished Boards
1st output percent →	90
2nd output destination →	Faulty Boards
2nd output percent →	10

Note that we must also enter the one resource into the Resource table and indicate there is only 1 available:

Name ↓	**Number available** ↓
R1	1

Exercise 17: Perform 20 simulations of an 8-hour work shift before and after the change. Report the overall mean <u>final</u> inventory of finished goods (i.e., the *throughput*) of the processes to assess the effect of the new machine.

Example 18: A machine with breakdowns

A factory has a metal stamping machine that is prone to breakdowns. Roughly 5% of the time, as the machine is being prepared for a new job, it gets jammed. Here is a process flow map of this situation using SimQuick elements:

Process Flow Map for a Machine with Breakdowns

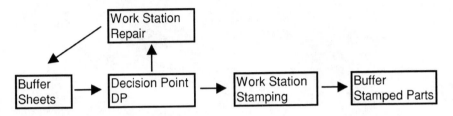

Objects representing the raw materials for this process are kept in the Buffer called Sheets. They next pass through a Decision Point where 95% of the time they go to the Work Station called Stamping and are processed as usual. However, 5% of the time they go to the Work Station called Repair. This corresponds to a breakdown of the stamping machine. We don't want any objects going to Stamping when this happens so we assign a common resource to the two Work Stations. The working time at Stamping can be approximated by a normal distribution with a mean of 1 minute and a standard deviation of .1 minutes. The working time at Repair can be approximated by a normal distribution with a mean of 10 minutes and a standard deviation of 2 minutes. Note that objects that leave Repair go back to Sheets because they have not really been processed yet (we assume they are not damaged).

Exercise 18:

a. Build a SimQuick model of the stamping machine process. Perform 20 simulation runs. Let time units represent minutes and run each simulation for 480 time units. Report the throughput (i.e., the overall mean <u>final</u> inventory in Stamped Parts).

b. The factory is considering investing in a new stamping machine. The new machine is advertised as working at the same speed as the old machine but with 98% reliability (repairs should take about the same amount of time as for the old machine). Using your model from part a, predict the throughput of the process using the new stamping machine.

Chapter 5: Project Management

Learning objectives:

- To model, simulate, and analyze projects with uncertain task durations
- To understand the effect of uncertain task durations on estimates of a project's duration

Overview

The techniques of PERT and CPM are widely used for managing complex projects. A weakness of these models is that they typically do not incorporate uncertainty when estimating the duration of projects (or, if uncertainty is included in the model, it is not handled in a realistic fashion). In this section, we show how uncertainty can be incorporated in the PERT/CPM approach by viewing a project as a process and applying the techniques of process simulation.

Example 19: A software development project

We consider a (very) simplified project for developing a software product, which is graphically described below. Each box represents a task (or activity) that must be completed. A task cannot be started until all its predecessors (tasks to its left) have been completed. Management wants an estimate of how long the project is going to take.

A standard technique for addressing this problem begins by estimating the duration of each task (with a single number). The next step is to identify the sequence of tasks from beginning to end (e.g., Design Software, Develop Interface, Begin Phase 2, Test/Debug, Produce/Release) whose sum of estimated durations is a maximum (the so-called *critical path*). This largest sum is an estimate of the project's duration.

A Software Development Project

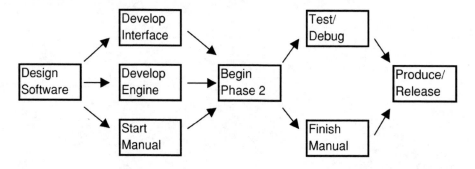

This technique does not capture an often crucial aspect of real projects; that is, task durations are typically uncertain and hence may not be modeled well by a single number. We propose to model projects with uncertain task durations using process simulation.

Modeling the process with SimQuick

The trick is to model each task with a Work Station. The arrows in the project diagram define the inputs and outputs of each Work Station in the usual fashion. The "Working times" of each Work Station are statistical estimates of the corresponding tasks' durations. These estimates are provided in the following table, which is followed by our SimQuick model.

Tasks	Task durations (days)
Design Software	Nor(20,5)
Develop Interface	Nor(50,10)
Develop Engine	Nor(55,10)
Start Manual	Nor(20,5)
Begin Phase 2	Nor(2,.5)
Test/Debug	Nor(20,5)
Finish Manual	Nor(20,5)
Produce/Release	Nor(30,8)

Buffers:

1

Name →	Start
Capacity →	1
Initial # objects →	1
Output destination(s) ↓	Output group size ↓
Design Software	1

2

Name →	End
Capacity →	1
Initial # objects →	0
Output destination(s) ↓	Output group size ↓

Work Stations:

1

	Name →	Design Software	
	Working time →	Nor(20,5)	
Output destination(s) ↓	# of output objects ↓	Resource name(s) ↓	Resource # units needed ↓
Develop Interface	1		
Develop Engine	1		
Start Manual	1		

2

	Name →	Develop Interface	
	Working time →	Nor(50,10)	
Output destination(s) ↓	# of output objects ↓	Resource name(s) ↓	Resource # units needed ↓
Begin Phase 2	1		

3

Name →	Develop Engine		
Working time →	Nor(55,10)		
Output destination(s) ↓	# of output objects ↓	Resource name(s) ↓	Resource # units needed ↓
Begin Phase 2	1		

4

Name →	Start Manual		
Working time →	Nor(20,5)		
Output destination(s) ↓	# of output objects ↓	Resource name(s) ↓	Resource # units needed ↓
Begin Phase 2	1		

5

Name →	Begin Phase 2		
Working time →	Nor(2,.5)		
Output destination(s) ↓	# of output objects ↓	Resource name(s) ↓	Resource # units needed ↓
Test/Debug	1		
Finish Manual	1		

6

Name →	Test/Debug		
Working time →	Nor(20,5)		
Output destination(s) ↓	# of output objects ↓	Resource name(s) ↓	Resource # units needed ↓
Produce/Release	1		

7

Name →	Finish Manual		
Working time →	Nor(20,5)		
Output destination(s) ↓	# of output objects ↓	Resource name(s) ↓	Resource # units needed ↓
Produce/Release	1		

8

Name →	Produce/Release		
Working time →	Nor(30,8)		
Output destination(s) ↓	# of output objects ↓	Resource name(s) ↓	Resource # units needed ↓
Counter	1		

9

Name →	Counter		
Working time →	200		
Output destination(s) ↓	# of output objects ↓	Resource name(s) ↓	Resource # units needed ↓
End	1		

Observe that we have added three additional elements. First, we have added a Buffer, called Start, that contains a single initial object and whose output is the first task of the project (in this case, Design Software). Second, we have added a Work Station, called Counter. It has a single input from the final task of the project (in this case, Produce/Release). Finally, we have added a Buffer, called End. It has a single input from Counter (and a capacity of 1).

The duration of the simulation is set to be some number of time units that exceeds the maximum possible duration of the project and the Working time of Counter is set to be the same number, in this case, 200 days. We run the simulation many times, say 100 times (the maximum allowed by SimQuick at one time).

Here is how the model works on our example. When a simulation begins, the object in Start immediately moves to Design Software. It stays there for an amount of time determined by our estimated duration of this task. After this, it is split into three objects, each of which goes to one of the outputs of Design Software. Each object stays at its Work Station according to our statistical estimate of these tasks' durations. Begin Phase 2 cannot start until it has one of each of its inputs; hence, it cannot start until each of its three predecessors is finished. The output of Phase 2 is two objects, each of which goes to one of its outputs. The same logic continues until Produce/Release sends one object to Counter. Due to our choice of "Working time" for Counter, the object will be worked on until the end of the simulation (we have the Buffer called End simply because SimQuick requires Work Stations to have an output). Because the "Working time" for Counter is equal to the duration of the simulation, we can calculate the duration of the project in this simulation as follows:

Project duration = (1 − fraction time working of Counter) * (Simulation duration)

To computer the overall mean project duration, simply substitute "overall mean fraction time working of Counter" for "fraction time working of Counter" in the above equation.

Exercise 19: Perform the following for the software production example above.

a. The duration of each task is described by a statistical distribution. If the duration of each task was precisely the mean of this distribution, what would the duration of the project be? (You do not need to use SimQuick, just find the longest sequence of tasks from the beginning to the end of the project.)

b. Report the overall mean duration of the project from 100 simulations of the above model (using the statistical distributions and SimQuick). How does this number compare with the duration reported in part a? Also report the maximum and minimum durations of the 100 simulated runs of the project.

Example 20: A house addition project

Consider the following house addition project.

A House Addition Project

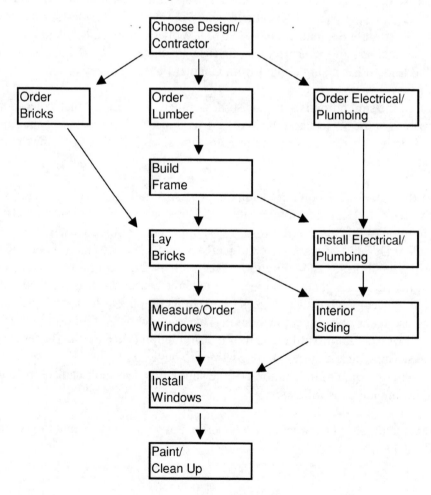

Tasks	Task durations (days)
Choose Design/Contractor	Nor(30,5)
Order Bricks	Exp(5)
Order Lumber	Exp(7)
Order Electrical/Plumbing	Exp(7)
Build Frame	Nor(2,.5)
Lay Bricks	Nor(2,.5)
Install Electrical/Plumbing	Nor(2,.5)
Measure/Order Windows	Exp(7)
Interior Siding	Nor(2,.5)
Install Windows	Nor(2,.5)
Paint/Clean Up	Nor(3,.5)

Exercise 20: Perform the following for the house addition example above.

a.   The duration of each task is described by a statistical distribution. If the duration of each task was precisely the mean of this distribution, what would the duration of the project be? (You do not need to use SimQuick, just find the longest sequence of tasks from the beginning to the end of the project.)

b.   Report the overall mean duration of the project from 100 simulations of the above model (using the statistical distributions and SimQuick). (Set the "Time units per simulation" and the "Working time" of Counter to 200 time units.) How does this number compare with the duration reported in part a? Also report the maximum and minimum durations of the 100 simulated runs of the project.

Appendix 1:
Enhancing SimQuick with Excel Features

In this appendix, we list ways to ease the use of SimQuick by taking advantage of some basic features of Excel.

Creating process flow maps

Process flow maps can be created in Microsoft Word or Microsoft Excel using the built-in drawing features. This section contains a description of the method used for the figures in this booklet; it's quick and dirty but gets the job done.

Begin by inserting a new worksheet into the SimQuick workbook with which you're working. To do this, click on "Insert/Worksheet" in the Excel menu. You can rename this new worksheet by double-clicking its tab at the bottom of the screen and typing a new name, say Flow Map.

Next, highlight any two cells, one above the other, in the new worksheet. On the menu, click on "Format/Cells." Then, click on the border tab. Choose a wide line width and the outline option. Click OK. The two cells should now have a border. Highlight these two cells again and, on the menu, click on "Edit/Copy." Now highlight any two cells in the worksheet where you want to place an element in your process flow map. From the menu, click "Edit/Paste." Repeat this to place all the elements in your map. To move a box, just highlight it and drag it to a new location. Now you can label each of the boxes with the element type and name. Finally, click on Excel's drawing icon in the menu, click on the black arrow icon, and draw arrows between the boxes.

Saving results

Suppose you have run a model and want to save some of the statistics from the Results worksheet. As discussed above, add a new worksheet to your SimQuick workbook by clicking on "Insert/Worksheet" in the Excel menu. Then, rename this new worksheet by double-clicking its tab at the bottom of the screen and typing a new name, say Saved Results. Copy any statistics from the Results worksheet that you want to keep and paste them into the new worksheet. Here is an example of a worksheet you might create for the bank example:

	A	B	C	D	E	F	G
1							
2	**Mean cycle times in teller line**						
3				**Simulation numbers**			
4		**Overall means**	**1**	**2**	**3**	**4**	**5**
5	One teller; no ATM	14.70	16.80	14.72	14.12	12.32	15.52
6	Two tellers	0.56	0.44	0.73	0.65	0.50	0.47
7	One teller; with ATM	8.61	8.23	13.80	9.86	5.47	5.67
8							

You are now ready to perform some statistical analysis of these results using the statistical capabilities of Excel. Some examples are provided below in the section, "Statistical analysis of SimQuick results."

Printing a model

The technique used in this booklet to print the tables in a SimQuick model is quite easy. For each element type, simply highlight one or two of the tables you have filled in, choose "Edit/Copy" from the Excel menu, and then "Paste" them into a Microsoft Word file (or the word processor of your choice). You can then add any labels and/or comments you like and print the result. Alternatively, you can simply add a new worksheet to your SimQuick workbook, paste the tables into it, and then print it.

Multiple SimQuick runs

Suppose you are running a SimQuick model several times but are not changing the underlying process flow map. For example, consider Example 8, where we study an "order-up-to" inventory policy at a grocery store. In part a of Exercise 8, you are asked to compute the service level for several different Storage capacities. This work can be reduced as follows.

As discussed above in the "Saving results" section, create a new worksheet in your SimQuick workbook and call it, say, InputOutput. Fill in the worksheet as follows:

	A	B	C	D	E	F
1						
2		Input storage cap.:	70		Storage cap.	Service level
3					70	
4					74	
5		Output service level:			78	
6					82	
7					86	
8					90	
9					94	
10						

In the cell C5, enter the formula: ='Results'!D19

For this model, this is the cell (on the Results worksheet) that, after each simulation, contains the overall mean service level at the Exit called Purchase Requests.

Next, go to the Buffers worksheet in SimQuick. It should look as follows:

	A	B	C	D
1	**Buffers**	Return to Control Panel		
2				
3	Examples			
4				
5				
6		1		
7		**Name** →	Storage	
8		Capacity →	70	
9		Initial # objects →	0	
10		Output	Output	
11		destination(s) ↓	group size ↓	
12		Purchase Requests	1	
13				

Enter the following formula into the cell that contains 70: ='InputOutput!'C2

The new workbook is used as follows. Go to the Control Panel and click Run Simulation(s). When the simulations are finished, go to the worksheet InputOutput. The cell C5 contains the overall service level from these simulations. Highlight this cell, click "Edit/Copy." Next, highlight the cell F3 and click "Edit/Paste Special." Click on "Values" and then OK.

Next enter 74 into C2 of the worksheet InputOutput, click Run Simulation(s) on the Control Panel. In the worksheet InputOutput, paste the contents of cell C5 into F4, as we did above. Continue in this manner.

This basic idea is particularly useful when a problem has more parameters to vary, as in Exercises 9, 10, and 11. Also, in these exercises, once you have collected all the statistics you need in InputOutput, you can easily perform the cost calculations all at once, using the basic calculating features of Excel.

Statistical analysis of SimQuick results

In this section, we consider three basic statistical calculations that can be performed on SimQuick results using the features of Excel. These calculations are made using the results from the individual simulations (this is the main reason this information is provided by SimQuick). Although we demonstrate how to perform the statistical analysis, we do not present the theory behind the statistics.

Let's reconsider the results from the original bank model in Section 1 of Chapter 2 for the element Line:

Element names	Statistics	Overall means	Simulation number(s)				
			1	2	3	4	5
Line	Objects leaving	55.20	57	54	54	55	56
	Final inventory	6.80	9	5	10	6	4
	Minimum inventory	1.40	1	2	0	2	2
	Maximum inventory	10.00	10	10	10	10	10
	Mean inventory	6.77	7.98	6.62	6.36	5.65	7.24
	Mean cycle time	14.70	16.80	14.72	14.12	12.32	15.52

Let's focus our attention on the mean cycle time. From our five simulations, SimQuick computed the following five numbers: 16.80, 14.72, 14.12, 12.32, and 15.52. These five numbers comprise a sample of mean cycle times from the population of all possible simulations of two hours using this model. (It is common practice to assume that such populations are approximately normally distributed; several of the calculations below depend on this assumption.)

Create a new worksheet called, say, Analysis1. A number of useful statistics can be obtained as follows. From the Analysis1 worksheet, click on "Tools/Data Analysis" on the Excel menu. (If Data Analysis does not show up in the menu, click on "Tools/Add-Ins" and then click the boxes next to Analysis Toolpack.) Highlight "Descriptive Statistics" and click on OK. Fill in the window as follows:

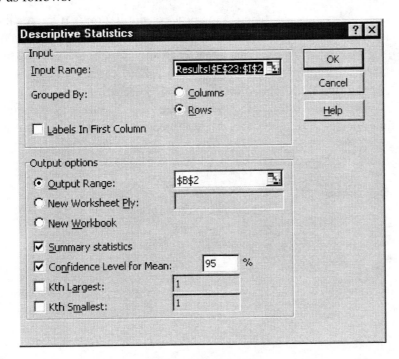

Note that the complete "Input Range" should read Results!$E$23:$I$23.

If you click on OK, the following table should appear in your worksheet:

	Row1	
Mean		14.70
Standard Error		0.74
Median		14.72
Mode		#N/A
Standard Deviation		1.66
Sample Variance		2.77
Kurtosis		0.47
Skewness		-0.34
Range		4.48
Minimum		12.32
Maximum		16.80
Sum		73.48
Count		5.00
Confidence Level(95.0%)		2.07

Note that the first row contains 14.70, the same mean that was computed by SimQuick in the cell Results!D23. A number of other statistics are also calculated; we consider only two of them. First, note that the standard deviation of the five numbers is 1.66, which tells us how "spread out" the five numbers are. Second, the last row provides us with a 95% confidence interval for the overall mean cycle time of the population. That is, there is a probability of .95 that the overall mean cycle time of the population is within 2.07 of 14.70 or, in other words, in the interval [12.63, 16.77].

Another common statistical question to ask when doing process simulation is if the results of a change in a model are statistically significant. For example, in the bank example, let's compare the mean cycle times in the Line when there is one teller, with and without an ATM. This calls for performing a t-test. Specifically, we want to know, at a .05 significance level, if the overall mean cycle time of the population in the "one teller with ATM" case is less than in the "one teller with no ATM" case. This is a known as a one-tailed hypothesis test. To do this, we copy the five mean cycle times for each case into a new worksheet called, say, Analysis2 as follows:

	E	F	G	H	I	J
1						
2	**Mean cycle times in teller line**					
3				Simulation numbers		
4		1	2	3	4	5
5	One teller; no ATM	16.80	14.72	14.12	12.32	15.52
6	One teller; with ATM	8.23	13.80	9.86	5.47	5.67
7						

Next, click on "Tools/Data Analysis" from the Excel menu. Highlight "t-Test: Two-Sample Assuming Unequal Variances" and click OK. Fill in the table as follows:

t-Test: Two-Sample Assuming Unequal Variances [dialog box]

Input
- Variable 1 Range: `$E$5:$J$5`
- Variable 2 Range: `$E$6:$J$6`
- Hypothesized Mean Difference: `0`
- ☑ Labels
- Alpha: `0.05`

Output options
- ⦿ Output Range: `$L$3`
- ○ New Worksheet Ply:
- ○ New Workbook

[OK] [Cancel] [Help]

Click on OK. The following table should appear in your worksheet:

t-Test: Two-Sample Assuming Unequal Variances		
	One teller; no ATM	One teller; with ATM
Mean	14.70	8.61
Variance	2.77	11.79
Observations	5	5
Hypothesized Mean Difference	0	
df	6	
t Stat	3.57	
P(T<=t) one-tail	0.01	
t Critical one-tail	1.94	
P(T<=t) two-tail	0.01	
t Critical two-tail	2.45	

We are interested in the number labeled "P(T<=t) one-tail," which is .01. Because this number is less than our significance level of .05, we may conclude the overall mean cycle time of the population in the "one teller with ATM" case is significantly less than in the "one teller with no ATM" case (with only a .05 probability that we are wrong; in fact, we would have drawn the same conclusion if we had set a .01 significance level). Hence, if our model is a good one, then adding an ATM machine in the real bank should significantly reduce the waiting time in the teller line.

Accelerating model entry

When entering a model into SimQuick that has several elements that are almost identical, use the ability of Excel to copy and paste ranges of cells. For example, consider Example 13, cellular manufacturing. Here we enter six Work Stations whose SimQuick tables are quite similar. To ease this entry, enter the table for WS1, then copy the range B7:D11 and paste it into cells G7, then L7, then Q7, then V7, and finally AA7. The desired tables for WS2 through WS6 can then be obtained with minor editing.

Appendix 2: Using Custom Schedules

In this appendix, we present an example of a process that uses a SimQuick feature called *Custom Schedules*. This feature allows the user to describe arrivals at Entrances and departures at Exits that cannot be described using SimQuick's statistical distributions.

Consider the following variation on the linear flow process in Example 12.

Process Flow Map for a Linear Flow Process with Custom Schedules

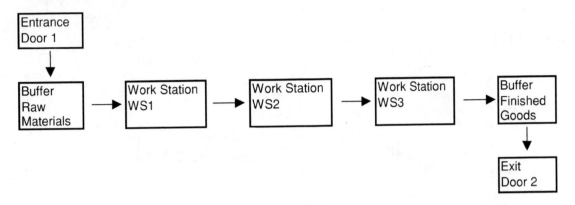

We let time units represent hours. There are 10 working hours per day and we want to simulate production for the next 100 days, so "Number of time units per simulation" is set to 1000. Additional details are provided below.

Entrances:

1	
Name →	Door 1
Time between arrivals →	Custom
Num. objects per arrival →	Custom
Output destination(s) ↓	
Raw Materials	

Exits:

1	
Name →	Door 2
Time between departures →	Custom
Num. objects per departure →	Custom

Buffers:

1	
Name →	Raw Materials
Capacity →	100
Initial # objects →	0
Output destination(s) ↓	Output group size ↓
WS1	1

2	
Name →	Finished Goods
Capacity →	100
Initial # objects →	0
Output destination(s) ↓	Output group size ↓
Door 2	1

Work Stations:

1			
Name →	WS1		
Working time →	Nor(5,1)		
Output destination(s) ↓	# of output objects ↓	Resource name(s) ↓	Resource # units needed ↓
WS2	1		

2			
Name →	WS2		
Working time →	Nor(5,1)		
Output destination(s) ↓	# of output objects ↓	Resource name(s) ↓	Resource # units needed ↓
WS3	1		

3			
Name →	WS3		
Working time →	Nor(5,1)		
Output destination(s) ↓	# of output objects ↓	Resource name(s) ↓	Resource # units needed ↓
Finished Goods	1		

Custom Schedules:

1	
Name →	Door 1
Time ↓	Quantity arriving/departing ↓
0	15
100	20
220	20
310	15
450	20
520	15
600	20
720	25
850	20
950	10

2	
Name →	Door 2
Time ↓	Quantity arriving/departing ↓
80	10
200	30
350	25
500	30
650	25
780	25
850	20
1000	15

Note that, for both the Entrance and the Exit, "Time between arrivals (departures)" and the "Num. of objects per arrival (departure)" are filled in with the word "Custom." This instructs SimQuick to look at the Custom Schedules tables (click on the "Custom Schedules" button on the Control Panel) for the arrival/departure schedules. These tables, shown above, are given the same name as the corresponding Entrance/Exit.

Consider the Custom Schedule table for Door 1. The table says that at time 0 (i.e., at the beginning of each simulation), 15 objects arrive at Door 1. Then at time 100, 20 more objects arrive, and so on. The table for Door 2 says that at time 80, 10 objects (or as many as are available) can leave the process from Buffer: Finished Goods. Then, at time 200, 30 more objects can leave, and so on. Such specific schedules are impossible to describe using SimQuick's built-in statistical distributions and, typically, are used to describe arrivals and departures that have been worked out in advance, or are being considered, with suppliers and customers. In this case, running this model may help you to estimate how well the schedule for your customers will be met by the arrival schedule of raw materials (i.e., What is the service level at Door 2?). If the service level is too low, you may, for example, have to reschedule some of the arrivals of the raw materials.

"Times" should be numbers between 0 and the "Number of time units per simulation." and they should increase as you move down in the table. Each "Quantity arriving/departing" should be an integer between 1 and 10,000. A Custom Schedule can contain up to 10,000 rows.

Custom Schedules can also be used to input into SimQuick arrival and departure schedules described by statistical distributions that are not built into SimQuick. Such a schedule must be generated with a different piece of software, put into the proper format, and then copied into a SimQuick Custom Schedule table.

Appendix 3: SimQuick Reference Manual

This appendix contains a concise description of all the features of SimQuick for reference. Methods for using SimQuick for modeling processes can be learned from reading Chapter 2, Section 1, and Chapter 3, Section 1.

Installing and running SimQuick

Please refer to Chapter 1, Section 4.

SimQuick Statistical Distributions:

A key feature of simulation software is a way to choose numbers randomly from statistical distributions. SimQuick provides the following formulas for doing this.

Nor(m,s)   Numbers are chosen from a normal distribution with mean = m, standard deviation = s.

Uni(a,b)   Numbers are chosen from a uniform distribution between a and b, with a < b.

Exp(m)   Numbers are chosen from an exponential distribution with mean m.

All numbers used in the above distributions must lie between .01 and 10,000.

The two uses for these distributions are for describing the working times at Work Stations and the arrival/departure schedules at Entrances/Exits. SimQuick also allows the arrival/departure schedules to be described with Custom Schedules (described below and in Appendix 2). With this feature, schedules described by (essentially) any distribution can be used, as well as any fixed schedule.

Note: SimQuick is "case sensitive"; hence, the three-letter abbreviations for the distributions must start with a capital letter.

Rules for all Elements

For each element in your model, you must fill in a table that describes the characteristics of that element. Each type of element has its own type of table. Blank tables can be found by clicking on the buttons on the Control Panel with the element type names. When filling in tables, be sure to fill in table 1, then table 2, and so on, without leaving any blank tables between two filled-in tables.

Note: SimQuick is "case sensitive"; hence, whenever a name for an element is entered into a table, it must be entered with the same upper- and lowercase letters.

Entrances and Exits

Entrances are where objects enter the model and Exits are where objects leave the model. If your model has several types of objects entering (perhaps they follow different paths through a job shop or are combined on an assembly line), then you should have a separate Entrance for each type. The same holds true if your model has several types of objects that leave (perhaps your model produces several different finished goods).

When filling in a table for an Entrance or an Exit, you must fill in the following cells:

1.   *Name* (must be distinct from names of other elements).
2.   *Time between arrivals (departures)* and *Num. objects per arrival (departure)*. These two cells define the arrival/departure schedule for the objects that arrive/depart at this Entrance/Exit. The choices for both are any one of the three SimQuick distributions or a number between .01 and 10,000.

   An additional choice is to write the word Custom into both cells. In this case, the arrival/departure schedule is described by the schedule you enter by clicking on the button Custom Schedules. The name of the Custom Schedule must be the same as the name of the corresponding Entrance/Exit (see Appendix 2).

When filling in a table for an Entrance, you must also fill in the following:

3.   At least one *Output destination* (in the top row). This is a list of the elements to which objects at this Entrance are sent. Don't leave any blanks in the middle of the list.

If objects arrive at an Entrance during the simulation, then as many as will fit enter the model. If there is not enough space for all of them, then those not entering are rejected from the model (they cannot enter at a later time).

If objects are scheduled to depart from an Exit during a simulation, then as many as are available at that time will depart up to the specified Num. objects per departure.

The following statistics are reported on the Results sheet for Entrances:

Objects entering process: This is the number of objects that arrived at the Entrance during the simulation and moved to one of its output destinations.

Objects unable to enter: This is the number of objects that arrived at the Entrance during the simulation but were unable to move to one of its output destinations (perhaps a Buffer was full or a Work Station was working).

Service level: This is equal to $\dfrac{\text{Objects entering process}}{\text{Objects entering process} + \text{Objects unable to enter}}$.

The following statistics are reported on the Results sheet for Exits:

Objects leaving process: This is the number of objects that leave the process at the Exit during the simulation (this typically represents filled demand).

Object departures missed: This is the number of objects that could have left the process at the Exit during the simulation but did not because they were not available at the inputs to the Exit (this typically represents unfilled demand).

Service level: This is equal to $\dfrac{\text{Objects leaving process}}{\text{Objects leaving process} + \text{Object departures missed}}$.

Buffers

Buffers simply hold objects. When filling in a table for a buffer, you must fill in the following cells:

1. *Name* (must be distinct from names of other elements).
2. *Capacity* (an integer between 1 and 10,000). This is the maximum number of objects that can be held at one time.
3. *Initial # of objects* (an integer between 0 and the capacity).

The following is optional.

4. *Output destination(s)*. This is a list of the elements to which objects at this Buffer are sent. If you fill in a row, you must fill in the top row. Don't leave any blanks in the middle of the list. The *Output group size* (an integer between 1 and 10,000) must be filled in for each output destination. This means that the Buffer groups together a specified number of objects before outputting them as a single object (e.g., if objects are put into boxes or sent to a machine as a batch). Hence, a Buffer will not send output to an element until it contains a multiple of the group size for that element.

If an output destination is not specified for a Buffer, then objects that enter the Buffer simply remain at the Buffer. Note that all objects entering a Buffer become indistinguishable. Hence, if you have two objects that represent different products, don't put them into the same Buffer.

The following statistics are reported on the Results sheet for Buffers:

Objects leaving: This is the number of objects that leave the Buffer and go to one of its output destinations during the simulation.

Final inventory: This is the number of objects in the Buffer at the end of the simulation.

Minimum inventory: This is the minimum number of objects in the Buffer during the simulation.

Maximum inventory: This is the maximum number of objects in the Buffer during the simulation.

Mean inventory: This is the mean number of objects in the Buffer during the simulation.

Mean cycle time: This is the mean amount of time that an object spends in the Buffer during a simulation. If no objects leave the Buffer during a simulation, then the mean cycle time is "Infinite."

Work Stations

Work is performed on the objects at Work Stations. When filling in a table for a Work Station, the following cells must be filled in:

1.   *Name* (must be distinct from names of other elements).
2.   *Working time.* This is the amount of work time per cycle. The choices are any one of the three SimQuick distributions or a number between .01 and 10,000.
3.   *Output destination(s).* This is a list of the elements to which objects at this Work Station are sent. If you fill in a row, you must fill in the top row. Don't leave any blanks in the middle of the list. For each output destination, you must specify the *# of output objects* (an integer between 1 and 10,000). (Use this, for example, when a Work Station breaks or disassembles an input into a number of outputs; typically, this number is 1.)

The following is optional.

5.   *Resource names.* This is a list of the resources that this Work Station needs in order to work. For each name entered, you must also enter the *# of units* of this resource that is needed (an integer between 1 and 10,000). Each resource used must also be entered in the table accessed by clicking on the "Resource(s)" button.

When a Work Station finishes working on an object, it will have created as many objects as designated for each output. It will retain these objects (in an internal buffer) until they have all been passed to subsequent elements in the model. The Work Station is *blocked* (i.e., it can perform no further work) until the created objects have all left the Work Station. Hence, for a Work Station to begin working, the following conditions must hold: the Work Station is not working; there is no finished inventory in the Work Station's internal buffer; there is one of each input object at each element providing the inputs; and, if resources are assigned to the Work Station, then the resources are available. When these conditions hold, the Work Station acquires one of each type of input object and the needed resources, determines the working time, and begins work. Resources are retained at the Work Station for the duration of the work; hence, they become unavailable to other Work Stations. When a work cycle is finished at a Work Station, its resources become available for reassignment.

Note that the requirement for a Work Station to have one of each input object before it starts processing allows a Work Station to model a machine whose work is to combine or assemble two or more objects.

The following statistics are reported on the Results sheet for Work Stations:

Final status: If the Work Station is working on an object at the end of the simulation, then its final status is "Working." Otherwise, its final status is "Not Working."

Final finished inventory: This is the number of finished objects in the internal buffer at the end of the simulation.

Mean finished inventory: This is the mean number of objects in the internal buffer during the simulation.

Mean cycle time (fin. inv.): This is the mean amount of time an object spends in the internal buffer during a simulation. It does not include time spent working on the objects.

Work cycles started: This is the number of times during the simulation that the Work Station has begun working on a new set of inputs.

Fraction time working: This is the fraction of the time during the simulation that the Work Station is working on an object.

Fraction time blocked: This is the fraction of the time during the simulation that the Work Station is blocked.

Decision Points

Decision Points route objects to one of two outputs. When filling in a table for a Decision Point, the following cells must be filled in:

1. *Name* (must be distinct from names of other elements).
2. Two *output destinations*: These are the elements to which objects at this Decision Point are sent.
3. Two *output percentages*: Both numbers must be between 0 and 100 and must add up to 100.

When an object enters a Decision Point, it is randomly sent to one of the two outputs based on the percentages. A Decision Point requires zero time and has a capacity of one object. Hence, a Decision Point can be *blocked* (i.e., it will not route any additional objects) if the unit it holds cannot go anywhere.

The following statistics are reported on the Results sheet for Decision Points:

Objects leaving: This is the number of objects that leave the Decision Point and go to one of its output destinations during the simulation.

Final inventory: This is the number of objects at the Decision Point at the end of the simulation. The number can be 0 or 1.

Resources

Each resource that is used must be listed in the resources table, which can be accessed by clicking on the "Resources" button on the Control Panel. It is also necessary to enter the number (or amount) of each resource that is available (an integer between 1 and 10,000). Resources are assigned to Work Stations in the corresponding tables (the number needed must also be specified: an integer between 1 and 10,000). Resources are useful for modeling situations where one person is operating several machines, where a machine has several setup configurations, and so on. The "Mean number in use" of each resource during each simulation is provided on the Results sheet. This can be used to assess the *utilization* of resources. Resources are used in Examples 6, 7, 13, 16, and 17.

Custom schedules

For each Entrance or Exit, arrival/departure schedules may be explicitly defined as Custom Schedules. When using this option for an Entrance or Exit, the word Custom must appear in the cells labeled "Time between arrivals/departures" and "# objects per arrival/departure." The specific schedule must be entered into a Custom Schedule table (click the "Custom Schedules" button). In these tables, the name of a Custom Schedule must be the same as the name of the corresponding element. "Times" are the specific times during the simulation when objects arrive/depart at the corresponding element. They should be numbers between 0 and the "Number of time units per simulation." and should increase as you move down in the table. Each time must be accompanied by a "Quantity arriving/departing," which represents the number of objects arriving/departing at that time. These should be integers between 1 and 10,000. A Custom Schedule can contain up to 10,000 rows.

A Custom Schedule can be used to model the arrival or departure of objects from the model according to a predefined schedule (see Appendix 2). This can also be used to model the arrival or departure of objects from the model according to a schedule that follows a distribution not built into SimQuick. Such a schedule must be generated outside of SimQuick and then copied into a Custom Schedule form.

Clearing the model

Clicking on the "Clear Present Model" button on the Control Panel clears all the SimQuick tables and the simulation control parameters.

Simulation control parameters

To run a simulation, you need to specify two numbers on the Control Panel. You must enter the *Number of time units per simulation* (a number between .01 and 100,000). This determines how long each simulation runs. A good strategy is to first choose what time units in the model represent in the real world so the arrival/departure schedules and the working times are relatively small numbers compared with the Number of time units per simulation. You also need to specify the *Number of simulations* (an integer between 1 and 100). Because the numbers used in the simulation are generated randomly, you can get different results each time you run the simulation. Thus, you may want to run the simulation more than once and perform some statistical analysis of the results.

To perform the simulation(s)

Click the "Run Simulation(s)" button.

Running time

SimQuick can take a few minutes to run if the number of time units is large, the number of simulations is large, and the number of elements is large. Running times will also depend on the speed of your computer. SimQuick updates the user on its progress in the lower right region of the Control Panel (and "beeps" when it finishes successfully). If SimQuick is not finished running after 30 seconds, a window appears and informs the user of SimQuick's progress. The user is given the option of stopping SimQuick or letting it continue. If the user elects to have SimQuick continue, then the user can specify a length of time. If SimQuick is not finished by this time, then this window reappears. SimQuick can be stopped at any time while running by hitting the Esc key.

Results

Results of any simulation run can be obtained by clicking on the "View Results" button on the Control Panel. The first two columns contain the element types and names in the SimQuick model. In the third column, the types of statistics collected during the simulations appear. Slightly different statistics are collected for each type of element. The statistics collected for each simulation are in the columns labeled 1, 2, 3, ... The final location of every object that arrived at the process (or started at a Buffer) can be determined as well as how many objects passed through each element. Other summary statistics are also available including statistics for Resources. Each number in the column labeled "Overall means" is the mean of the five numbers to its right. (For details, see "Rules for all elements" earlier in this appendix, or Example 1 in Chapter 2.)

Additional model limits

At most, a model can have 20 of each type of element, 10 outputs from an element, and 20 resources. (There is no additional restriction on the number of inputs to an element.)

How each simulation is performed

When a SimQuick simulation begins, a "simulation clock" starts in the computer and runs for the designated duration of the simulation. While this clock is running, a series of *events* sequentially takes place. There are three types of events in SimQuick: the arrival of a shipment of objects at an Entrance, the departure of a shipment of objects from an Exit, and the finish of work on an object at a Work Station. Whenever an event occurs, the elements are scanned a number of times in the order of their *priority*: Entrances before Work Stations before Buffers before Decision Points before Exits; and, subject to this, in increasing order of table numbers.

A special purpose of the first scan is to consider the resources: If a Work Station has just finished working, then its resources become available and its newly finished objects become available to subsequent elements. Resources are not reassigned until the second scan (hence, a high-priority Work Station may reacquire its resources immediately after completing work). After the first scan, elements (except Entrances) attempt to "pull in" objects from their input elements. If a Buffer, Decision Point, or Exit has more than one input element, then it will attempt to pull in objects from its input elements in priority order. Methods for using the notion of priority in modeling are discussed in Examples 7, 16, and 17.